MW00709848

GUNS

Tools of Destructive Force

These and other books are included in the Encyclopedia of Discovery and Invention series:

Airplanes
Anesthetics
Animation
Atoms
Automobiles
Clocks
Computers
Genetics
Germs
Gravity
Guns
Human Origins
Lasers
Microscopes
Movies
Phonograph
Photography
Plate Tectonics
Printing Press
Radar
Radios
Railroads
Ships
Submarines
Telephones
Telescopes
Television
Vaccines

GUNS

Tools of Destructive Force

by DEBORAH HITZEROTH

The ENCYCLOPEDIA of
D•I•S•C•O•V•E•R•Y
and **INVENTION**

P.O. Box 289011 SAN DIEGO, CA 92198-9011

Printed in the U.S.A.

Library of Congress Cataloging-in-Publication Data

Hitzeroth, Deborah, 1961-
Guns: tools of destructive force / by Deborah Hitzeroth.

p. cm.—(The Encyclopedia of discovery and invention)
Includes bibliographical references and index.
Summary: Describes the different types of guns and traces their history, social importance, and future.
ISBN 1-56006-228-2 (alk. paper)
1. Firearms—Juvenile literature. [1. Firearms.] I. Title.
II. Series.
TS533.H58 1994
683.4'09—dc20 93-19130
CIP
AC

Contents

Foreword 7

Introduction 10

CHAPTER 1 ■ Propelled by Fire 12

Early weapons;
Explosive powder;
Fire tubes and hand cannons.

CHAPTER 2 ■ The First Guns 20

The mechanical firing power of the matchlock;
The wheel lock;
The flintlock's superior firing system.

CHAPTER 3 ■ Far-Reaching Effects 32

Guns on the battlefield;
Dinner on the table;
A new means of protection;
Early gun control laws;
Dueling.

CHAPTER 4 ■ The Rifle 40

Building a better gun;
The Kentucky rifle;
A new bullet improves accuracy;
Improved loading and firing techniques.

CHAPTER 5 ■ The American West 54

The pepperbox pistol;
The Colt wins the West;
The revolver goes west;
A pocket-sized pistol.

CHAPTER 6 ■ Rapid-Fire Guns 63
Guns for a new era;
Machine guns go to war;
World War II introduces the submachine gun.

CHAPTER 7 ■ Antiaircraft Guns 75
Combating airborne threats;
Guns that never were;
Radar's magic eye.

CHAPTER 8 ■ The Future 82
Faster firing;
Smarter weapons;
Automatic targeting and firing;
Into the next century.

Glossary 87
For Further Reading 88
Works Consulted 89
Index 91
About the Author 95
Picture Credits 96

Foreword

The belief in progress has been one of the dominant forces in Western Civilization from the Scientific Revolution of the seventeenth century to the present. Embodied in the idea of progress is the conviction that each generation will be better off than the one that preceded it. Eventually, all peoples will benefit from and share in this better world. R.R. Palmer, in his *History of the Modern World*, calls this belief in progress "a kind of nonreligious faith that the conditions of human life" will continually improve as time goes on.

For over a thousand years prior to the seventeenth century, science had progressed little. Inquiry was largely discouraged, and experimentation, almost nonexistent. As a result, science became regressive and discovery was ignored. Benjamin Farrington, a historian of science, characterized it this way: "Science had failed to become a real force in the life of society. Instead there had arisen a conception of science as a cycle of liberal studies for a privileged minority. Science ceased to be a means of transforming the conditions of life." In short, had this intellectual climate continued, humanity's future would have been little more than a clone of its past.

Fortunately, these circumstances were not destined to last. By the seventeenth and eighteenth centuries, Western society was undergoing radical and favorable changes. And the changes that occurred gave rise to the notion that progress was a real force urging civilization forward. Surpluses of consumer goods were replacing substandard living conditions in most of Western Europe. Rigid class systems were giving way to social mobility. In nations like France and the United States, the lofty principles of democracy and popular sovereignty were being painted in broad, gilded strokes over the fading canvasses of monarchy and despotism.

But more significant than these social, economic, and political changes, the new age witnessed a rebirth of science. Centuries of scientific stagnation began crumbling before a spirit of scientific inquiry that spawned undreamed of technological advances. And it was the discoveries and inventions of scores of men and women that fueled these new technologies, dramatically increasing the ability of humankind to control nature—and, many believed, eventually to guide it.

It is a truism of science and technology that the results derived from observation and experimentation are not finalities. They are part of a process. Each discovery is but one piece in a continuum bridging past and present and heralding an extraordinary future. The heroic age of the Scientific Revolution was simply a start. It laid a foundation upon which succeeding generations of imaginative thinkers could build. It kindled the belief that progress is possible as long as there were gifted men and women who would respond to society's needs. When Antonie van Leeuwenhoek observed *Animalcules* (little animals) through his high-powered microscope in 1683, the discovery did not end there. Others followed who would call these "little animals" bacteria and, in time, recognize their role in the process of health and disease. Robert Koch, a German bacteriologist and winner of the Nobel Prize in Physiology and Medicine, was one of these men. Koch firmly established that bacteria are responsible for causing infectious diseases. He identified, among others, the causative organisms of anthrax and tuberculosis. Alexander Fleming, another Nobel Laureate, progressed still further in the quest to understand and control bacteria. In 1928, Fleming discovered penicillin, the antibiotic wonder drug. Penicillin, and the generations of antibiotics that succeeded it, have done more to prevent premature death than any other discovery in the history of humankind. And as civilization hastens toward the twenty-first century, most agree that the conquest of van Leeuwenhoek's "little animals" will continue.

The *Encyclopedia of Discovery and Invention* examines those discoveries and inventions that have had a sweeping impact on life and thought in the modern world. Each book explores the ideas that led to the invention or discovery, and, more importantly, how the world changed and continues to change because of it. The series also highlights the people behind the achievements—the unique men and women whose singular genius and rich imagination have altered the lives of everyone. Enhanced by photographs and clearly explained technical drawings, these books are comprehensive examinations of the building blocks of human progress.

GUNS

Tools of Destructive Force

GUNS

Introduction

Throughout history, humans have used the gun as a tool for protecting and providing for themselves. But the gun is more than a simple tool, and its effect on humanity has been dramatic. The gun leaves behind a mixed legacy, one marked both by noble causes and shameful acts. To the dedicated—and well-armed—citizen soldiers who fought for an independent United States, the gun represented freedom. Yet the gun has also been used by despots to prevent people from achieving freedom.

Thus the gun, morally neutral in and of itself, can be used to aid or destroy. For our ancestors, who relied on a successful hunt for much of their food, the gun raised the odds of survival. For many people today the gun provides a sense of security, a means of protection in a confusing and sometimes dangerous world. Yet the gun is also the favored tool of those who seek to dominate others. Whether in distant nations or in our own neighborhoods and

TIMELINE: GUNS

1 2 3 4 5

1 ■ 1240
Roger Bacon experiments with black powder, later adapted for use as gunpowder.

2 ■ 1326
The fire tube, the first instrument to use black powder to launch projectiles, is used in war.

3 ■ 1380s
The hand cannon, a fire tube adapted for mobility and use by individual soldiers, is invented.

4 ■ 1411
Invention of the matchlock musket, the first true gun with a mechanical firing device.

5 ■ 1510
The wheel lock, a gun that could fire in any kind of weather, is used in war.

6 ■ 1610
Invention of the flintlock, the most superior musket-firing system ever produced.

7 ■ 1780s
Rifling technique introduced by German immigrants.

schools, the gun is used to carry out senseless murders and maimings.

The triumphs and tragedies associated with the gun underscore, perhaps more than other inventions, the complex nature of the human mind. For human ingenuity alone has the capacity to invent an essentially simple instrument possessing such deadly force. And only the human mind can find such disparate purposes for its inventions.

The gun's invention and its refinement did not come about all at once. In this respect it is like many other inventions; its development has ranged over many centuries and has grown from the minds of many inventors. This process of invention and refinement goes on today as does the dual nature of the gun, and both are likely to continue far into the future.

7 8 9 10 11 12 13 14

8 ■ 1805
Development of the percussion cap, which replaced loose gunpowder as a propellant.

9 ■ 1835
Samuel Colt introduces revolvers.

10 ■ 1855
The minié ball improves speed and ease of loading rifles.

11 ■ 1862
Richard Gatling demonstrates his newly invented machine gun.

12 ■ 1865
Breech-loading weapons begin to replace muzzle loaders.

13 ■ 1884
H.S. Maxim builds first machine gun that relied totally on mechanical means for rapid fire.

14 ■ 1936
Germany builds first antiaircraft gun.

15 ■ 1990
U.S. government improves PHALANX gun designed to protect naval ships from aircraft and missile attacks.

CHAPTER 1

Propelled by Fire

In many ways the history of guns has paralleled the history of warfare. As people have needed new weapons that could strike faster, harder, and farther, guns have evolved to meet these needs. The history of this evolution is long and colorful. Even though no one knows who invented the first gun—an instrument that could strike a target from a long distance with great force while keeping its user safely out of harm's way—historians do have some idea of how they developed.

Like many inventions, guns did not come about all at once. Rather, they evolved slowly over a period of centuries. The idea for the first gun probably grew out of an earlier weapon designed to strike from a distance, the crossbow. Bows and arrows were among the first weapons that allowed hunters and warriors to strike at their targets over long distances with great accuracy and force. The crossbow's most important feature was a lever or crank that drew the bow taut. Once drawn, the lever held the string tight until the user was ready to fire. Because this weapon used a mechanical device to store energy, it could be considered a step toward the development of guns. All previous weapons depended on the user's strength and stamina to hold the weapon ready for firing. Before the crossbow physical strength had been the basis of power. With the invention of weapons like the crossbow and later the gun, might no longer depended on physical strength.

The crossbow allowed hunters and warriors to strike their targets from a distance.

The transition from the crossbow to the gun was made possible by gunpowder, the explosive substance that gave guns their deadly force. The idea for gunpowder probably came from the days when Europe was first beginning its trade with Asia. Thirteenth-century merchants and traders sailed across vast oceans in search of goods that would bring high prices in the European markets and make them wealthy. They brought silks, spices, and many curiosities from the Far East. Among these items were fireworks.

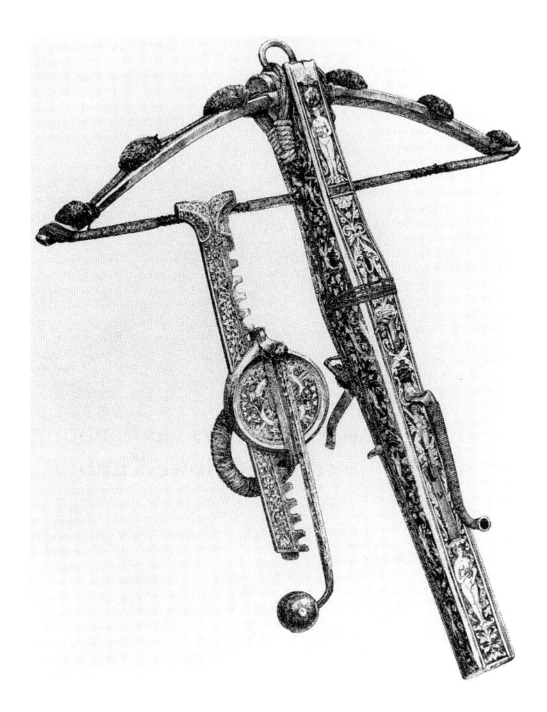

The crossbow required less physical strength than previous weapons, because a lever or crank drew the bow taut.

In with a Bang

Fireworks were a tradition in China. Many centuries back, possibly as far back as one thousand years, Chinese entertainers, religious leaders, and citizens set off fireworks to commemorate and celebrate important events. During most celebrations and religious festivals, the bright flashes and loud bangs of fireworks filled the air. These celebrations no doubt attracted the attention of European traders, who always kept an eye out for goods with money-making potential. Thus, fireworks made their way from Asia to the European continent along with many other exotic items. Although the wealthy classes clamored for these unusual goods, public reaction to fireworks did not exactly warm the hearts of the eager merchants. Most people, when they saw the flash of light and heard the terrible noise, believed the explosion was caused by witchcraft. They feared that anyone who used the fireworks was a sorcerer or witch who had made deals with the devil.

While the general public feared the fireworks, European inventors and scientists took an immediate interest in the fireworks and the explosive black powder within them. Their experiments revealed that the powder's composition was simple and easy to reproduce. It consisted of three fairly common ingredients: saltpeter, or salt crystals, sulphur, and charcoal. These ingredients were ground into a fine powder and then mixed by hand.

As scientists worked with the mixture, the knowledge they gained spread slowly across the continent. By the early 1200s the black powder was known across Europe. The first European to write about making this powder was Roger Bacon, an English philosopher and scientist. Around 1240 Bacon wrote about the mixture that "produce[d] a lightning flash and noise of thunder." Bacon, a noted scientist of his time, was curious about the explosive mixture. He wanted to know what made the powder explode.

Like the general public, however, leaders of the Catholic church regarded the powder as black magic. In 1139 the church had "laid under anathema [cursed] any person who made fiery compositions [substances]." This meant that anyone who used the black powder or experimented with it risked imprisonment or death. Knowing this, Bacon conducted his experiments in secret. Even though he avoided discussing his work, word of his experiments spread.

His work eventually became public knowledge and led to his imprisonment. Church officials believed Bacon was practicing witchcraft and in 1257—ten years after he became a Franciscan monk—imprisoned him in a Paris monastery. He remained there, isolated from the world, for nine years.

Although Bacon's research came to a halt, other researchers had embarked on their own studies of black powder. Word of their work spread, and educated people began to understand that the powder had nothing to do with witchcraft. When Bacon was released from the monastery in 1266, he resumed his studies and began writing about what he knew best—science.

(Above) Scientist and philosopher Roger Bacon experimented with explosive powder and saw its potential for use in warfare. (Below) A seventeenth-century engraving depicts a step in the process of producing gunpowder. Prior to this time, the explosive powder was thought to have been a product of witchcraft.

Workers refine saltpeter, one of the ingredients used in making the explosive black powder used in fireworks.

Among the topics that captured his attention was black powder. Bacon's writing hints that people were beginning to consider using the explosive mix in warfare:

> From the flaming and flashing of certain igneous [fiery] mixtures and the terror inspired by their noise . . . which no-one can guard against or endure. . . . These compositions can be used at any distance we please, so that the operators escape [any injury] from them, while those against whom they are employed are suddenly filled with confusion.

Despite Bacon's clear allusion to the black powder's potential for use as a tool of war, historians think several decades may have passed before this idea actually took hold. The process may have been hastened by an accident involving black powder, a barrel, and a German monk.

According to one unconfirmed story, a fourteenth-century German monk called Berthold Schwarz ignited a small amount of black powder in a closed barrel. When the powder exploded, the container's lid was thrown high into the air. This probably occurred because black powder is transformed into a hot gas in a fraction of a second when it is burned. The expanding gas produces a shock wave that

Berthold Schwarz is credited with the idea of using explosive powder to forcefully project an object from inside a tube.

slams against surrounding surfaces and blasts objects from its path. From this experiment, Schwarz is said to have developed the idea of enclosing the powder in a tube and using the powder's explosive force inside the tube to propel an object.

Schwarz's experiments apparently came to an early end, however. One day, while mixing a batch of explosives, Schwarz is said to have caused a massive explosion that killed him and blew his monastery to fragments. Historians may never know for sure what happened in Schwarz's laboratory that day. What they do know, however, is that the explosive ability of black powder had been discovered by the world's military powers by the 1300s. Records show that a device called a fire tube was being used in war as early as 1326.

Fire Tubes

The fire tube is considered the earliest ancestor of the gun because it was the first instrument to use black powder's explosive force to hurl projectiles at distant targets. This weapon looked like a large metal vase laid on its side. The fire tube's base was fixed to a large board to hold it in place. Black powder was packed into the tube through the muzzle, or front, followed by an arrow or rock. If an arrow was used, a strap of leather was wrapped around its shaft to make it fit snugly into the vase. Once the arrow or rock was in place, the fire tube was aimed toward its target and the powder was ignited through a small hole near the back called a touch hole. When the powder exploded, it created a great amount of force. As the force escaped from the tube, it pushed the arrow or rock out of the tube's muzzle.

There are various reports of fire tubes being used in war. One of the earliest was a brief mention in 1331 in Florence city records of the tubes being used in Italy to repel attackers. The tubes were also used by the French to fire arrows against the English in 1340. Following the attack by France, the English were quick to build fire tubes of their own. An account of the Battle of Crécy in 1346 says that the English king Edward III "struck terror in the French Army with five or six" fire tubes. The fire tubes caused French soldiers to flee from the battlefield in panic. Many soldiers who heard the loud explosions and witnessed the billowing smoke succumbed to superstitious beliefs that were common at the time. The smoke and noise, they feared, were caused by demons summoned by their enemies.

Rumors circulated on the battlefield that those who controlled the fire tubes had made deals with the devil.

Many soldiers fled the battlefield rather than face an unseen enemy. Those who stayed to fight felt powerless to defend themselves against the arrows and rocks launched so forcefully from the fire tubes. The force behind these weapons could cause them to pierce armor and shields, something that was not possible with other types of weapons. In addition, the noise of the explosions often caused the horses to panic. This placed added danger in the path of soldiers who now also faced the threat of being trampled by frightened horses.

Even though the fire tubes seemed like invincible weapons to the soldiers facing them, these weapons had many problems and even posed a danger to those who used them. Materials in the Middle Ages were crude, and the weapons poorly made. Often the tubes exploded after only a few firings, killing anyone standing nearby. And even those tubes that held up through a number of firings were not very effective.

The force of the explosion of early black powder was relatively weak compared to the force of modern gunpowder, so targets could be no farther than a few yards away. In addition, the weapons were hard to aim. When an arrow launched from a fire tube hit its target, it was more by chance than skill. The fire tubes took a long time to load and fire and were too heavy and bulky to be moved easily. Where they were placed at the beginning of a battle was

Along with crossbows and longbows, English soldiers at the Battle of Crécy used fire tubes against the French. Fearing these new weapons, many French soldiers fled from the battlefield in panic.

where they remained throughout the conflict. Soldiers needed a lighter, more mobile weapon.

Hand Cannons

Some of these problems were solved around 1381 by the invention of the hand cannon. Unlike fire tubes, which were large and unwieldy, hand cannons were small enough to carry.

The hand cannon consisted of a six-foot-long iron tube encased in two hollowed-out pieces of wood tied together with rope. The wooden cover protected the gunner's hand from the tube, which became very hot when fired. Like the fire tube, this weapon was loaded from the muzzle and lighted by a match through the touch hole in the top of the tube. To fire the hand cannon, a gunner clamped it between one arm and his body then inserted a red-hot wire into the touch hole with the other hand.

Because the hand cannon weighed only fifteen to twenty-five pounds, it could be carried around the field during battle. This weapon was first used by German soldiers from the town of Augsburg in a battle against a group of southern German nobles. While it was an improvement over the simple fire tube, the hand cannon was still inaccurate and hard to load and fire. The most inconvenient thing about these early weapons was their firing system. To shoot a fire tube or hand cannon, soldiers had to have a hot iron or fire nearby.

Toward the end of the fourteenth century part of the hand cannon's problem was resolved by the slow

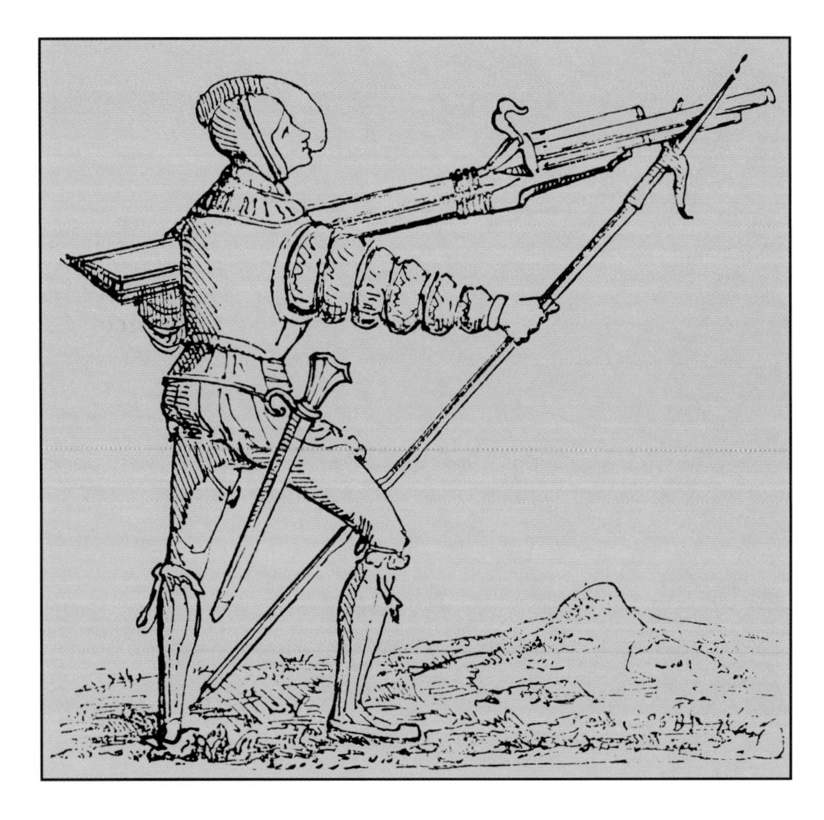

The hand cannon was light enough to carry and improved on previous weapons, but it was still inaccurate and hard to load.

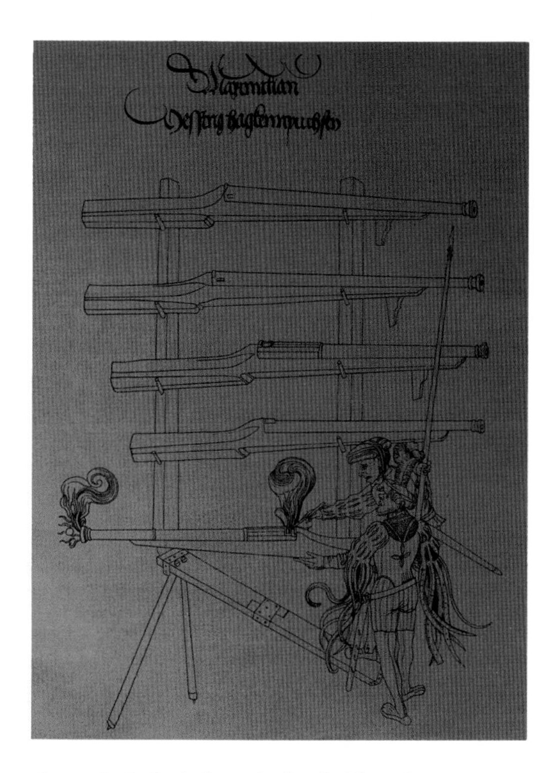

An artist's depiction of a loaded hand cannon being fired. A red-hot wire is inserted into the touch hole to set off the charge.

match. This was a length of loosely woven hemp cord that was coated with a saltpeter mixture. When the cord was lit, it would smoulder slowly and the burning end could be used to ignite the hand cannons and fire tubes. With the development of the slow match, gunners could move around the battlefield more freely.

The slow match improved the efficiency of hand cannons, but they were still difficult to operate. Besides being awkward to hold, light, and fire, they required a soldier's full attention. The soldier had to keep an eye on the touch hole while lighting it instead of watching the target. Later adjustments made the hand cannon easier to use. The rear was widened so that soldiers could rest it against their shoulders instead of holding the weapon under their arms. This wide end became known as the stock. The touch hole was moved from the top of the weapon, where it was exposed to the wind, to the side, where it was protected from the wind. These improvements helped make the weapon easier to fire and use, but they did not solve all of the problems. Loading and firing a hand cannon was still a slow and awkward process.

Soldiers needed a weapon that would fire quickly and accurately and allow them to keep their eyes on the enemy. This weapon, which would eventually come to be known as the gun, would be the essential tool of war. Within a matter of decades this new weapon would also contribute to political upheaval and social change. And, in this way, the gun would influence the course of human history.

CHAPTER 2

The First Guns

The names of the inventors of the first guns are lost in time. Historians are not even sure which country first developed guns, although Germany usually receives credit. Even though we do not know the names of the early inventors, the transformation from the awkward, match-lit hand cannons to sleek-barreled, mechanically fired guns—called muskets—is recorded for history.

Muskets

This transformation began at the end of the fourteenth century with the improvements being made to hand cannons. By the early fifteenth century, hand cannons had given way to muskets. The musket was simply constructed. It consisted of a long, hollow, metal tube called a barrel. The barrel had an opening at one end. This is where the musket was loaded, and it is also where the ammunition or projectile emerged. Loading the musket involved tightly packing the barrel with gunpowder. This was done with a long stick called a ramrod. The tightly packed powder gave the charge more force. Once the powder was packed, a rounded stone or ball of lead, brass, iron, or bronze, called shot, was rammed inside.

The musket also had a stock for holding and steadying the weapon. What primarily set it apart from weapons of previous eras was the mechanism that controlled firing—a mechanical firing device. With this development the act of firing was reduced to the mere pressure of a finger. Muskets were faster to use and easier to fire than any previous weapons.

The matchlock musket was built in about 1411. It takes its name from its firing mechanism, also called a matchlock. Primitive though it was, the matchlock musket was better than anything else yet developed. Its firing system is relatively simple. It consists of an S-shaped piece of metal that extends

The matchlock musket's mechanical firing device allowed the user to fire with the pressure of just a finger.

THE MATCHLOCK MUSKET

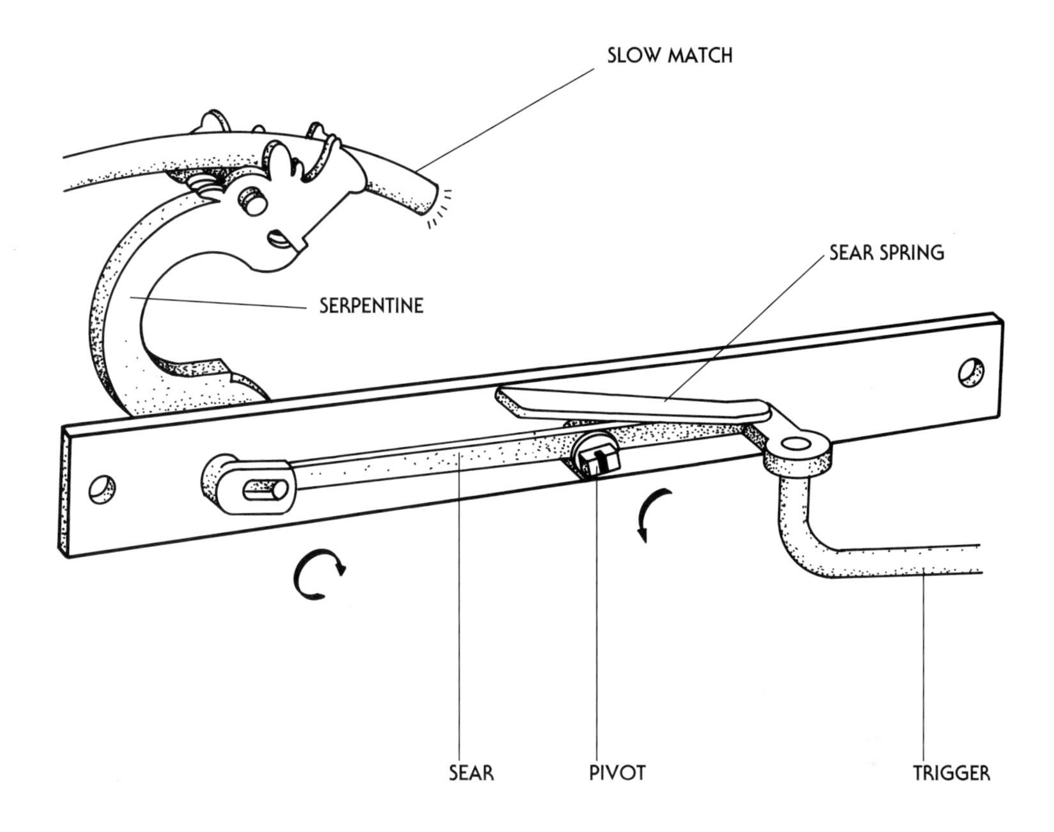

The first spring-powered mechanically fired gun was the matchlock musket. Although it weighed a lot and loading was slow and dangerous, the matchlock remained in use for more than two hundred years.

The matchlock firing mechanism is a simple mechanical device. The user locks a burning slow match into a curved holder, or serpentine. The serpentine is held in a raised position, clear of the pan which holds the priming powder, by an arm or sear and a small spring, called a sear spring. Pressure on the trigger releases the sear which turns on a pivot. The motion of the sear pushes the serpentine downward until the glowing match makes contact with the powder in the flash pan and ignites the charge. When the musketeer releases the trigger, the sear spring once again pushes down on the sear, returning the serpentine and slow match to the starting position.

A close-up view of a seventeenth-century German matchlock musket shows the firing mechanism of the gun.

above and below the barrel. The portion below the barrel is called the trigger; the portion above holds a segment of lighted slow match. When the user pulls the trigger, the slow match dips through a slit, or lock, into a depression in the barrel. This depression, or priming pan, holds a small amount of gunpowder. The slow match quickly ignites the powder in the priming pan, causing an explosion that ignites the gunpowder inside the musket. The force of the explosion inside the musket then propels the shot or stone from the gun toward its target.

The greatest advantage of these early guns is that a soldier or hunter could aim and fire the gun at the same time. Once the gun was loaded, the user could align the barrel and squeeze the trigger, all the while keeping an eye on the target. This sounds like only a small improvement, but it made a big difference in the odds of hitting a target. Instead of watching the gun in order to fire it, the soldier could watch the target.

But the matchlock musket was far from being the ideal weapon. The priming powder, or gunpowder in the priming pan, easily spilled out of the gun. Wet weather made the priming powder useless, and sparks from the slow match often ignited the priming powder before the gunner was ready to fire. To remedy these problems a cover was placed over the priming pan. The cover slid forward during loading and firing to protect the gunpowder from spilling, sparks, and rain.

Another drawback to the matchlock system was its lack of speed. It often took several seconds for the slow match to dip into the priming pan and ignite the gunpowder. In an effort to make the matchlock musket fire more rapidly, the snapping matchlock, or "serpentine," was developed. In this gun the simple S-shaped lever was replaced by a curved match holder, called a serpentine, driven by a spring. The match holder was drawn back and held by a spring. When the trigger was pulled, the holder was released and flew forward under the pressure of the spring, lighting the powder in the priming pan.

The matchlock musket was also plagued by some of the same problems as its ancestors. Rain could extinguish the burning slow match and render the gun useless. If a soldier waited too long to fire the gun without adjusting the slow match, it would burn back to the serpentine and go out. In addition to being easily extinguished, the burning end of the slow match made gunners vulnerable to an enemy's attack at night. The glowing slow match clearly marked a soldier's position, and enemies could easily evade a sentry by watching the glow of his gun as he walked.

Another problem with these early guns is that they often exploded after a few firings. James II, king of Scotland, was a victim of the matchlock musket. In 1460 during the siege of Roxburgh Castle, on the Scottish-English border, the king stood too close to a gun when it was fired. The gun exploded and James was "stricken to the ground and died [nastily]," according to reports of the battle.

Wheel Lock

Working to solve some of these problems, inventors developed another firing mechanism, which came to be known as the wheel lock. Like the matchlock, the wheel lock inventor's name is lost to history. Some historians credit the wheel lock's invention to the Italian artist Leonardo da Vinci because of drawings he did around 1508. These drawings show a mechanical firing sys-

The wheel lock's firing mechanism consists of a wheel which revolves against a piece of stone. Friction between the wheel and stone creates sparks which fall into the priming pan and ignite the gunpowder. A close-up view of the seventeenth-century wheel lock pictured below appears at left.

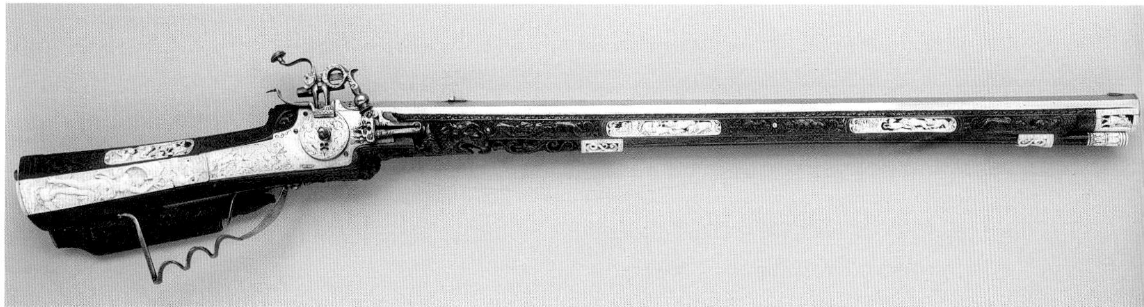

WHEEL LOCK

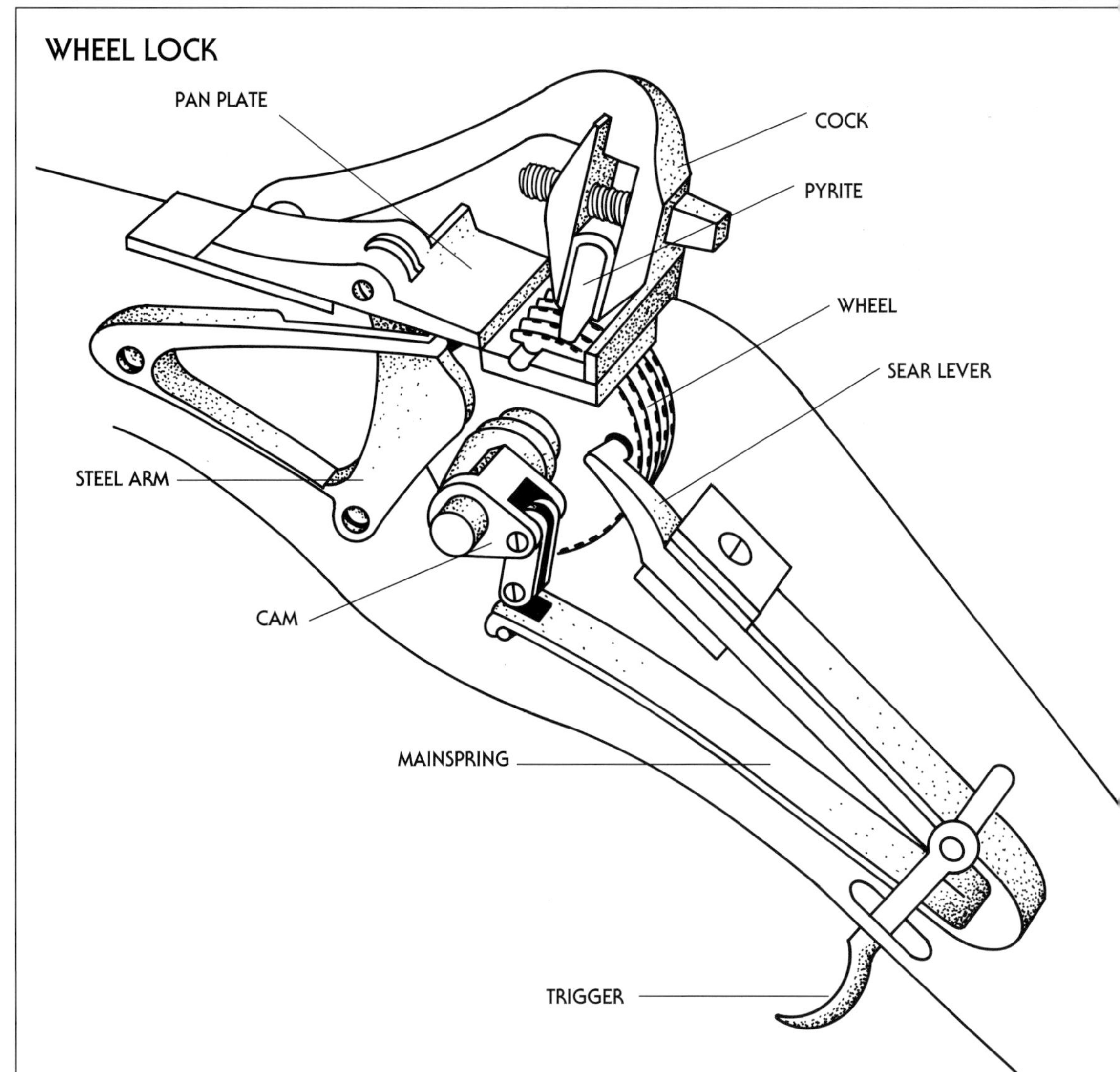

The wheel lock design solved many of the problems associated with the matchlock. It was easier to ignite, safer to use, and more reliable in damp and windy weather than the matchlock.

In the wheel lock the gunpowder in the pan is shielded from wind and rain by the pan plate. A moveable arm known as a cock holds a piece of pyrite, a mineral that emits sparks when struck by metal. The cock raises and lowers above a toothed wheel. The wheel is attached to a mainspring. The end of a spring-loaded lever, known as the sear lever, fits into the wheel and keeps it from spinning until the trigger is pulled. Pressure on the trigger releases the sear lever, causing the wheel to rotate quickly. As the wheel turns, it moves a cam. The cam strikes a steel arm, which opens the pan plate. At the same time, the teeth of the moving wheel grind against the pyrite, creating a spark. The spark ignites the priming powder, which in turn ignites the main charge.

tem similar to the early wheel lock systems. But other historians believe that Leonardo's drawings had more imaginative than practical value and could not have led to the invention of the wheel lock. Other historians credit German clock makers with the invention of the wheel lock because the intricate wheels in the gun were often built by clockmakers. While it is unclear who invented the device, it was in use by 1510.

The wheel lock firing mechanism, which relied on friction rather than the slow match, was superior to the matchlock because it could operate in any kind of weather. The wheel lock used a serrated wheel that revolved rapidly against a piece of stone, usually flint. The action of the wheel revolving against the stone caused sparks to fall into the priming pan and ignite the gunpowder. When the gun was fired, the cock, a hinged arm holding a piece of iron, was pulled forward against the wheel. Pulling the trigger released the wheel, allowing it to spin rapidly against the stone. Pulling the trigger also slid the pan cover open so that sparks could fall into the priming powder.

Even though they were more effi-

At the time of its invention, the wheel lock was too expensive for common use. Only kings, nobles, and wealthy merchants could afford them. Often these guns were elaborately decorated and inlaid with gold and silver. Shown here are three views of a seventeenth-century Swiss wheel lock. Clockwise from top left are a close-up view of the firing mechanism, a view of the design on the gun butt, and a full view of the gun.

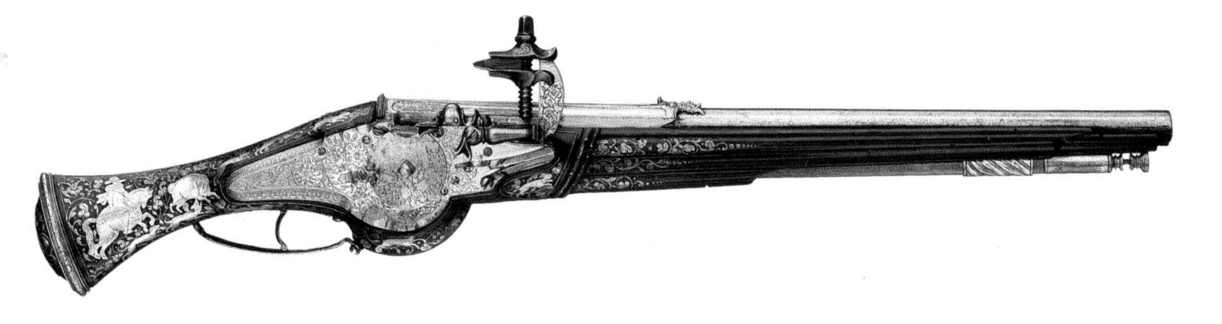

A double-barreled wheel lock pistol designed especially for King Charles V about 1540 was crafted from steel, gold, wood, and bone.

cient than matchlocks, wheel locks did not immediately catch on. The complex firing mechanism added to the cost of building the guns, and many armies deemed them too expensive to make. Also, every part of the wheel lock had to be put together very precisely. Unlike a matchlock weapon, which could be repaired by any blacksmith, wheel locks had to be repaired by specially trained craftsmen. If a wheel lock broke during battle, it was useless until a craftsman could be found to repair it. Armies were unwilling to spend the necessary amount of money to buy and repair the new wheel lock muskets, so they stuck with the cheaper matchlock guns. The average wheel lock, which cost about two years' wages, was too expensive for most people; only kings, nobles, and wealthy merchants could afford them.

Although the wheel lock muskets were used for hunting, they were prized for their craftsmanship. Some wheel locks of the 1500s and later were decorated with ivory, mother-of-pearl, gold, and silver. Panoramic scenes from Greek and Roman myths were carved into the wooden stocks. King Charles V of Spain and Archduke Ferdinand of Austria both owned wheel locks. According to palace records, Charles once paid the equivalent of about sixty years' wages for a common laborer to a Vienna gunsmith for a set of two wheel lock pistols. This was an unheard of amount of money, even for most royalty.

Snaphaunce

For decades wheel locks remained too expensive for common use. But between 1550 and 1585 an invention that has been credited to both Holland and Germany made the wheel lock system affordable for military use. Known as the "snaphaunce," the firing mechanism derived its name from either the Dutch phrase *snap Haens* meaning "hen thief" or the German term *schnappahn* meaning "snapping hammer." According to Dutch legend, this quiet and efficient gun received its name because it was a favorite weapon of chicken thieves. According to German legend, it was named for its quick-firing action. Historians are not sure which story is true.

This gun was an improved version of the wheel lock and had a simpler design. In the snaphaunce musket a moving stone was brought into contact with a fixed wheel when the trigger was pulled. The firing mechanism was a spring-loaded arm, called the cock, which carried a piece of flint at its tip. This system was easier and cheaper to construct than the original wheel lock system, making it more practical for military use. The invention quickly spread, and soon most European countries were building their own versions for army use. The Spanish added a new feature, called the half-cock position, and called their invention the Spanish lock. In the Spanish lock, a second bolt was used to hold the hammer in position after it was pulled back. The Spanish lock held the gun cocked and ready to be fired but kept it from accidently firing. This enabled soldiers to load and cock their guns in advance and have them ready to fire when needed. The snaphaunce quickly became popular with both common citizens and the military. Here finally was a gun that was accurate, reliable, economical to build, and could be used in rainy weather without access to fire or slow match.

Flintlocks

The snaphaunce musket remained popular until the early 1600s, when it was replaced by the flintlock firing system. The invention of this mechanism is usu-

An early seventeenth-century snaphaunce pistol has simple lines and an absence of ornate decoration, but its firing mechanism is an improvement over the wheel lock.

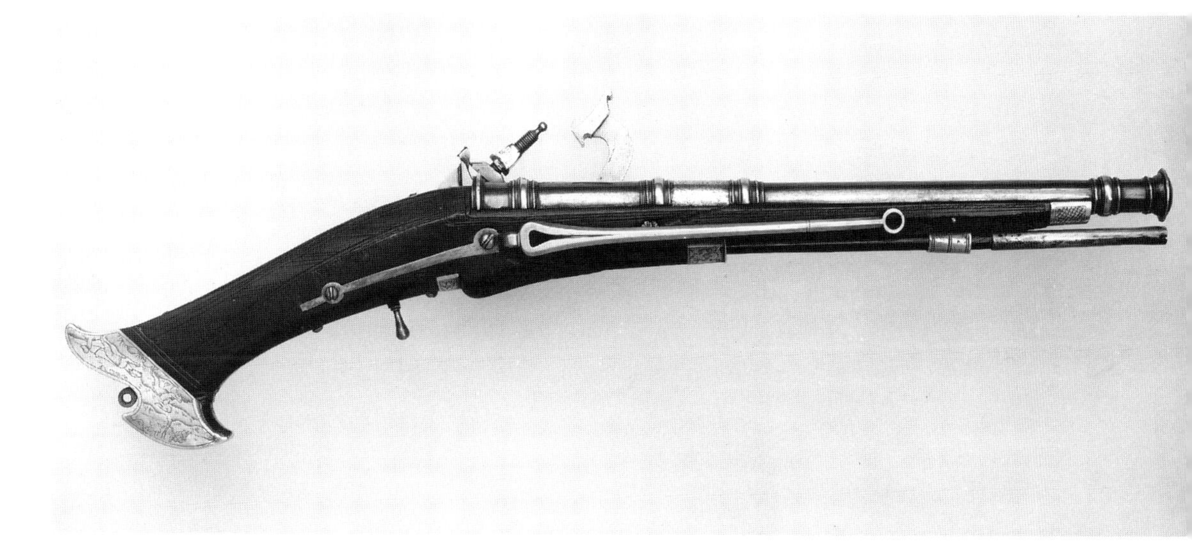

FLINTLOCK

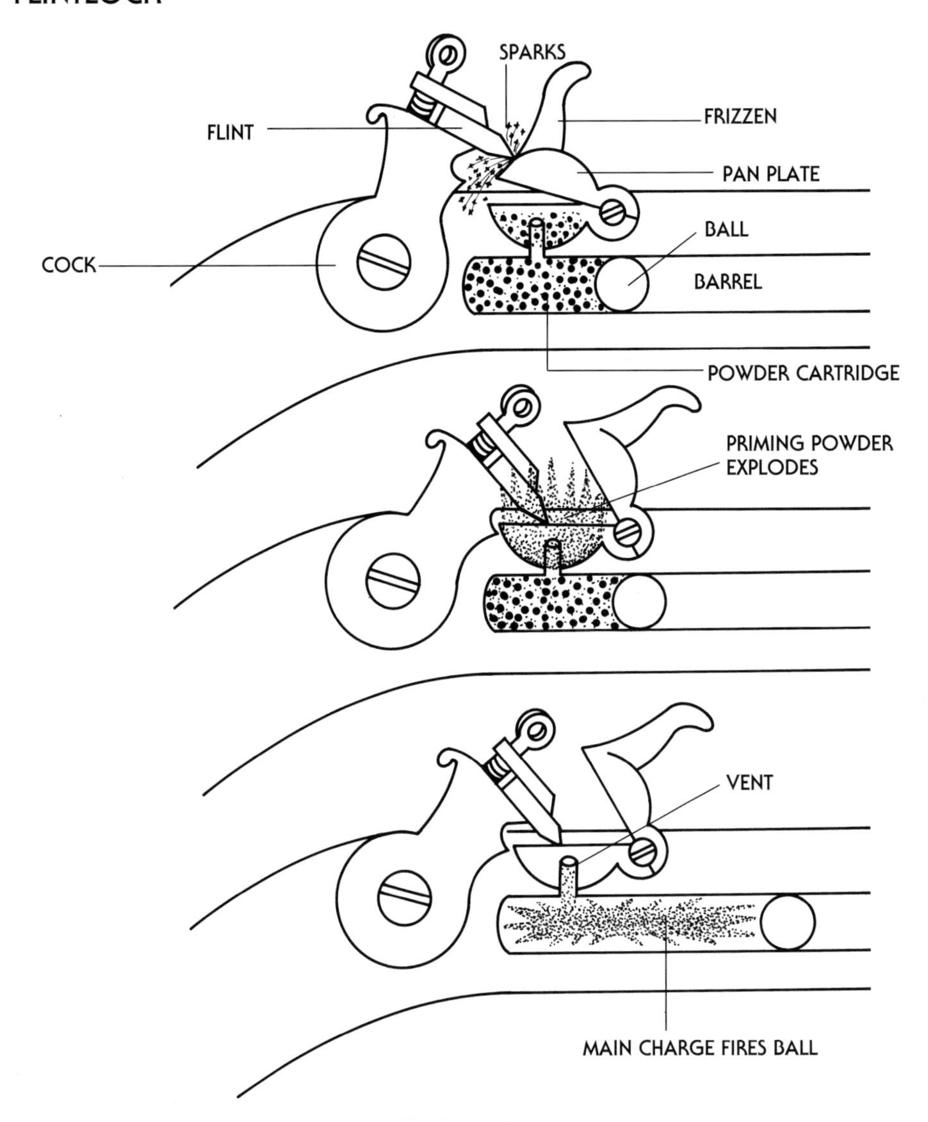

Like the wheel lock, the flintlock uses contact between roughened steel and a mineral to create a spark that ignites the priming powder. The flintlock design is much simpler than the wheel lock, however. The spring-loaded cock of the flintlock holds a small piece of flint in its jaws. Pressure on the trigger releases the cock, causing it to spring forward. The flint strikes a piece of roughened steel known as the frizzen, which is connected to the pan plate. As the flint slides down the face of the frizzen, it creates a cascade of sparks. At the same time, the pressure of the flint against the frizzen causes the pan plate to open. The shower of sparks falls into the priming powder, causing it to explode. The flame from the explosion passes through a vent igniting the main charge.

ally credited to Marin le Bourgeoy who was the gunmaker to King Louis XIII of France. This firing system, which was faster and more reliable than any before, first appeared between 1610 and 1630. Like the earlier Spanish matchlock, the flintlock had both a cocked and half-cocked position. The entire firing mechanism was enclosed in a lock plate, which protected it from the weather. The flintlock had all of the advantages of the rapid-firing wheel lock and snaphaunce weapons, but it was a much simpler mechanism, so it was cheaper to produce.

The French military quickly adopted this gun because it was simple to operate, inexpensive to produce, and reliable to use. In 1660 King Louis XIV of France equipped five regiments with this gun, making it the official gun of France. News of this firearm spread throughout Western Europe, and by 1700 it was the premier musket in use.

The flintlock (left) was fast, reliable, and inexpensive. A close-up view (below) shows details of the firing mechanism.

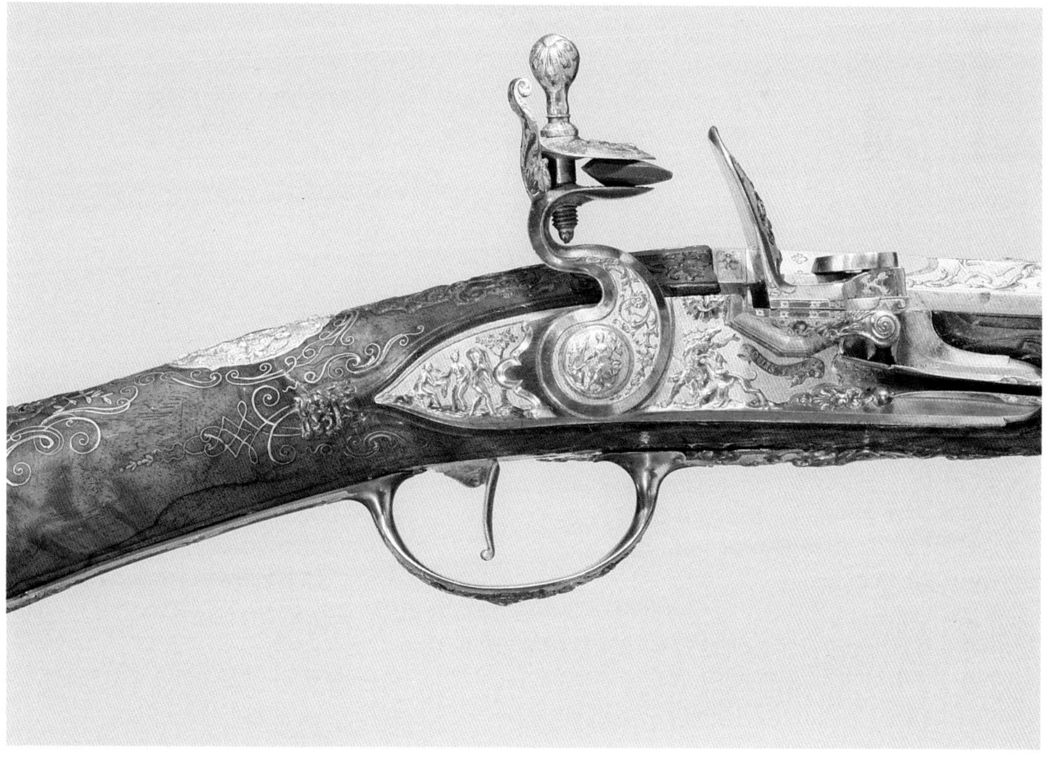

The Gun King

The flintlock firing system was a vast improvement over earlier guns, but soldiers still complained that the musket was hard to load and carry. These problems were soon solved by a young king who used firearms to turn his small country into a powerful nation. King Gustav Adolph II, who ruled Sweden from 1611 to 1632, created the world's first national army and equipped his soldiers with flintlocks, which were the best firearms available. Despite their reputation, Gustav knew the flintlock could stand some improvements.

One of the chief problems was that reloading took a long time. To reload, soldiers had to carefully measure out a shot's worth of gunpowder, pour it down the muzzle of their gun, insert a metal ball, and ram the gunpowder tightly into the muzzle. For inexperienced gunners this process could be agonizingly slow. During one battle in Germany the slowest soldiers were said to have fired their weapons only seven times in eight hours.

To speed the loading process Gustav invented the paper cartridge. The paper cartridge held a metal ball, to be used as a bullet, and a premeasured amount of gunpowder. When a soldier was ready to fire, he bit off the end of the paper cartridge, poured a small amount of the powder into the flash pan, and the remainder into the gun's muzzle. Then he simply wadded up the paper cartridge, with the bullet still inside, and rammed the whole thing into the gun. This method simplified loading and firing because the gunner no

Ornate seventeenth-century wheel locks with stocks of ivory reveal that guns were prized for their artistic craftsmanship as well as their ability to perform.

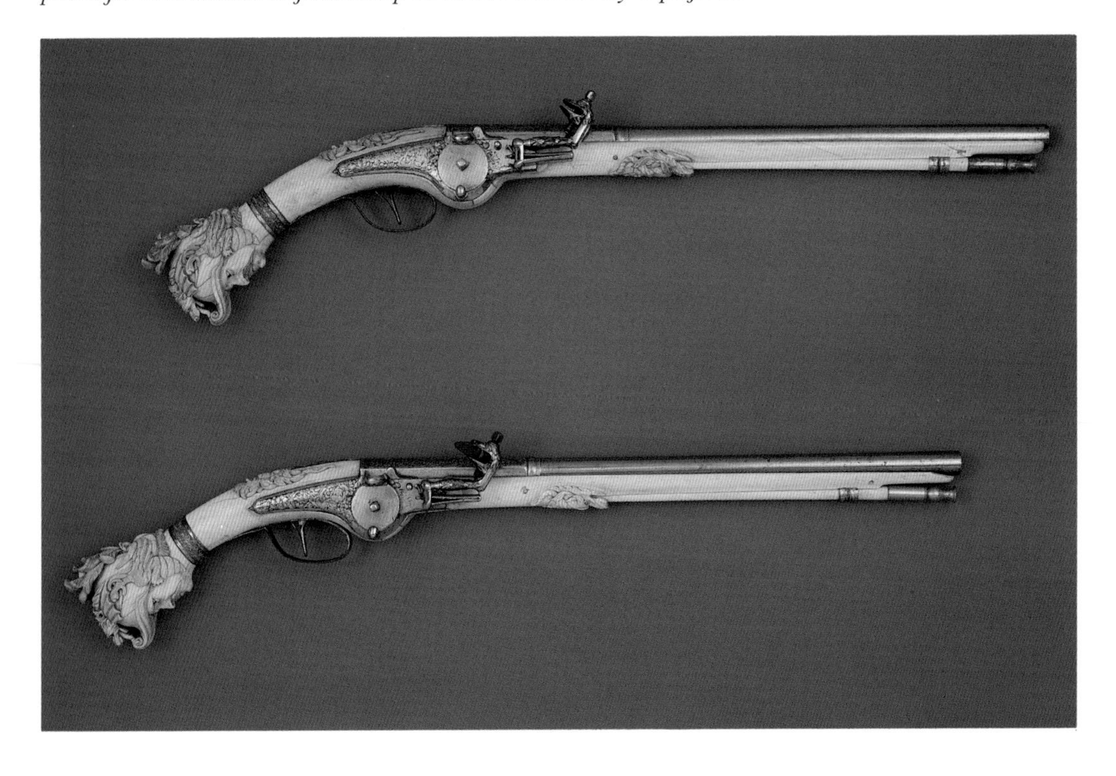

Flintlock guns are displayed with other weapons in an armory.

longer had to measure the amount of gunpowder required. The paper cartridge allowed Swedish troops to fire three times faster than before. Experienced soldiers could fire up to one shot a minute using these cartridges.

Soldiers also complained that muskets were too heavy to carry on long marches. To solve this problem, Gustav hired English gunsmith Robert Scott. Seeking to lighten the gun, the two men attempted to make gun barrels out of copper cylinders banded with iron and tied together with leather cords. These guns were lighter, but they did not hold up well. After only a few shots the barrels often exploded. The men never found a durable lightweight material, so they settled for shortening the gun barrels instead. By doing this Gustav was able to trim the musket's weight from twenty-five pounds to eleven pounds.

Using these new, quicker loading, and lighter weight weapons, the Swedish troops were formidable foes. They quickly developed a reputation for being effective and deadly marksmen. Guns had become an integral part of warfare. They would also change human society forever.

CHAPTER 3

Far-Reaching Effects

Since their invention, guns have been viewed as both a weapon of evil and a powerful conveyer of social change. Guns drove knights from the field of battle and killed the era of chivalry. They gave power to the physically and politically weak and aided in the formation of new nations. Above all else, guns elevated human conflict to new, deadlier levels.

War

One of the most obvious changes guns brought about in their early years was on the battlefield. Most soldiers dreaded facing gunfire in battle. As guns became more accurate, they also became more deadly, and the wounds they left were devastating. Even a minor bullet wound often caused death. The bullets carried vermin and germs from a soldier's clothes, and, after penetrating the skin, sealed the germs into the wound. And, while an arrow could be pulled from a wound fairly easily and the wound washed out, bullets usually had to be removed by surgery. Fifteenth- and sixteenth-century doctors did not sterilize their instruments, so surgery often caused massive infections that killed the patient.

In order to protect themselves from

The era of armored knights came to an end with the invention of the gun.

Although swordsmen and archers needed expertise to be successful on the battlefield, unskilled peasants could quickly learn to fire a musket.

the deadly gunfire, many soldiers carried magic amulets and potions. Astrologers sold charts that showed when the stars were the most favorable for war and when a person was most likely to sustain injury from a gunshot. While conjurers, or wizards, grew rich by providing these services, soldiers continued to die on the battlefield.

Guns changed warfare in other ways too. Before the invention of guns, wars were won by heavily armored knights who bore bows and arrows, swords, maces, and lances. Guns gradually replaced these weapons and eventually knights, too, disappeared from the battlefield. Initially, the knights rejected guns as a legitimate tool of war. They viewed guns as the weapons of cowards. Instead of fighting face to face with an enemy, a gunner struck from a distance. Many knights thought that guns had no place in civilized society. As one French soldier wrote in 1547, "no use has yet been made in France . . . of that terrible weapon against men. The French used it with some good effect against some castles . . . but they would [not] employ it against their fellow-creatures."

The anonymous French soldier's words were soon outdated. By 1563 guns were widely used in battle. That year Italian soldier and scholar Piernio Belli wrote *Treatise on War and the Military*, in which he explained that guns had become common on the battlefield. Belli also lamented the invention of such a deadly weapon. He wrote:

> Firearms of a thousand kinds are the most common and popular implements of war, as if too few avenues of death had been discovered in the course of the centuries, had not the generation of our fathers, rivalling God with his lightning, invented this means whereby even at a single stroke men are sent to [death] by the hundreds.

The changes wrought by guns on

the battlefield had far-reaching effects for whole societies. Peasants, members of the lower classes, had long served the knights and nobles. On the battlefield they carried supplies, pulled wagons, and dug ditches. They took no part in the fight, however, for this was viewed as the sole province of the upper classes. This arrangement changed with the appearance of guns on battlefields around the sixteenth century.

Even the most unskilled peasant could be taught to fire a matchlock. While it took years to make an expert swordsman or archer, it took only a few weeks for someone who had never used a gun to become a passable shooter. Healthy peasants were no longer viewed simply as beasts of burden, but as potential soldiers. And, for the first time, these soldiers were given special privileges that had been reserved for the wealthy.

By the mid-1500s artillerymen, soldiers who specialized in using guns, received an extra month's pay for each fortress captured or siege repelled. Gunners were served dinner before other soldiers, and they did not have to wait in line for food like the others. These soldiers were also allowed to have their families travel with them, something that had not been allowed in the past.

Guns also helped break the ties binding peasants to their fields. After being trained to use a gun, many peasant soldiers did not return to their fields. They had new skills to sell, and they were highly sought after by warring kings and rich cities. Between wars peasants who were trained in the use of guns often became mercenaries, or soldiers who were for hire by any army that needed them. Over time roving bands of mercenaries evolved into a sort of professional army. Living in groups that ranged from a few hundred to a few thousand, these armies were loyal only to their captains rather than to any particular nation, noble, or king. Peasants were no longer tied to their land and their liege lord, the nobleman to whom the peasant owed allegiance; instead, they were free to live and serve who they wanted. These mercenary soldiers wielded tremendous military power.

Dinner on the Table

Those soldiers who did return to their farms brought their knowledge of guns with them. Slowly guns began to trickle from military into civilian life. Firearms provided a better way for poor farmers

A hunter rests with gun in hand and dogs at his side. Guns helped people provide food for themselves and their families.

to put food on the table than had any earlier weapon.

In the early 1500s English peasants began using guns to hunt game on land belonging to the nobility. This act, called poaching, was a serious crime. While the landowners might not miss a few birds or a deer killed by a farmer's bow and arrow, they did notice the large number of animals killed by the poachers' guns. In some areas the wildlife was hunted almost to extinction.

In an effort to stop the flood of peasant hunters from gunning down wild game, King Henry VII enacted a series of laws in 1508 that made illegal the unlicensed use of guns. In 1515 his son, King Henry VIII, enacted even tougher laws that made it illegal for anyone with an income of less than two hundred pounds a year to own a gun. This was an amount close to two years' wages for most people. This law disqualified 93 percent of England's population of five million people. The law was intended to allow only the wealthiest citizens to own a gun. But all of these laws failed. The English people, having found an effective way to keep their families fed, refused to give up their guns. By the mid-1500s most of these laws had been repealed or were universally ignored by nobles and commoners alike, and guns continued to become more a part of daily life.

To prevent game hunting on royal land, King Henry VIII made it illegal for most people to own guns.

Armed and Dangerous

Guns offered a new type of protection for travelers who were physically weak or unskilled in the use of swords or bows. In the past these wayfarers were at the mercy of any robber they encountered. Guns helped to even the odds in a difficult situation.

But armed civilians sometimes posed a problem for local government officials. Arguments often escalated into public shootings. One newspaper recounted the story of two friends whose argument over a slight matter grew into a fatal gun battle. According to the story, they "were of a sudden . . . the most violent enemies in nature, breathing nothing but Death and Destruction. . . . [Then] there was a dying man reflecting on the rashness of what he had done, how trifling and vain had been the dispute that had [caused] his death."

In an effort to stop the reckless use of guns, cities began passing ordinances to outlaw them. In 1522 the Italian city

LOADING THE MATCHLOCK

1

2

The proper method of loading the matchlock was described in *The Management of Arms, Arquebuses, Muskets and Pikes* by Jacob de Gheyn, which was first published in Amsterdam in 1608. The book contains 116 engravings illustrating all aspects of matchlock care and use. Gheyn's book was considered the foremost authority on musketry for nearly eighty years. This period ended when the flintlock replaced the matchlock as the most innovative gun.

In Gheyn's day, a musketeer was not considered properly dressed and ready for action unless he wore certain items. Hanging from the bandolier draped around his upper body, a musketeer often carried two dozen wooden cartridges, or gun powder containers. In addition, a musketeer always carried spare lengths of slow match, a small flask for priming powder,

5

3

4

6

a bullet pouch, and a rapier or sword.

The six engravings shown here are from Gheyn's book. They depict the proper technique for loading a matchlock musket. In the first, the musketeer opens a wooden gunpowder cartridge with his thumb. In the second, he pours the gunpowder down the barrel of the musket; readying it for the bullet. In the third picture, he uses a ramrod to push the bullet down the barrel until it rests firmly on the gunpowder. In the fourth, he pours priming powder from a flask into the priming pan. Note that in his left hand the musketeer holds the slow match, which is already burning. In the fifth illustration, he blows the ashes off the slow match before locking it into place above the priming pan. The final illustration shows the musketeer, his matchlock supported by the forked rest stick, aiming, and firing.

of Ferrara passed laws forbidding anyone to carry a gun without authorization. These laws also established the penalty for violating the law. One law said:

> Since an especially dangerous kind of firearm has come to be used . . . with which a homicide can easily be committed; . . . knowing that these are devilish arms, [the city] prohibits . . . their being carried . . . without explicit authorization under penalty of having a hand publicly cut off.

The Italian cities of Milan and Florence quickly followed Ferrara's lead, according to a government proclamation, "because these arms are being used more and more for murders and assassination."

Dueling

These early gun control laws failed, too. Like their English neighbors, the Italians refused to abandon their firearms. Instead of falling out of use when they were outlawed, guns continued to become more ingrained in society. Guns eventually became such an accepted part of society that they were no longer thought of as weapons of the devil; rather, they became weapons of honor. In the seventeenth century dueling with guns became a popular way of settling questions of honor among the English and French nobility.

During this time in England the number of deaths by dueling reached a thousand people a year. According to tradition, a duel is a fight between two people over a matter of honor. The definition of what was considered a matter of honor varied widely from person to person. There was one case of a French nobleman who fought fourteen duels over the question of which French poet was the best. Later this same nobleman admitted that he had never even read any of the poems for which he had killed men. In a duel, the challenger—the person who felt his honor had been

Charles Dickinson falls to his death, after exchanging shots in a duel with Andrew Jackson.

Duels were a quick method of settling disagreements. Shown here is the famous duel between Aaron Burr and Alexander Hamilton, in which Hamilton was mortally wounded.

hurt—would demand satisfaction for some real or imagined insult. The person he challenged had the choice of accepting the duel or being marked a coward, a label that would cost him social standing and friends.

Duels were usually held in secret locations because in most countries killing someone during a duel was considered murder. During the duel the two opponents would face each other at a distance of about thirty feet apart and fire their weapons. If neither person was killed during the first round of shooting they were allowed to fire again. Not all duels were fatal. After the first round of shots either party could end the duel. But in many cases the duels were fought to the death.

The tradition of dueling lasted for centuries in Europe and eventually spread to the Americas, where many prominent men engaged in the practice. One of the most famous duels involved a man who would survive to become a U.S. president, Andrew Jackson. In 1806 Jackson and his opponent Charles Dickinson faced each other on the "field of honor," as the dueling area was called. Dickinson's bullet struck the future president in the chest and broke one of his ribs. Jackson was lucky to receive only a broken rib. A few inches lower, and the bullet would have missed the rib and entered his heart. Dickinson was not as lucky, for Jackson's shot proved to be fatal.

The fact that even a future president accepted gun duels as a valid method of settling an argument shows how widely accepted guns had become in society. Before reaching this point, however, guns underwent some important changes.

CHAPTER 4

The Rifle

In 1642, during the English civil war, peasants used flintlock and matchlock muskets to force King Charles I from his throne. Few English citizens had believed that this could actually happen. But the muskets proved to be deadly weapons in the hands of the farmers and peasants whose hunting skills had grown over time. The victorious peasant army showed the world that a band of poor but determined people could defeat highly trained royal troops if they had the proper weapons. American colonists later obtained similar results in their many battles for freedom from British rule during the American Revolution.

Although the American Revolution was fought successfully with the same style of muskets that the English peasants had used a century earlier in the English civil war, the colonists soon saw a need for a better weapon. The musket was a powerful gun, but loading was slow and sometimes dangerous. The soldier had to be standing to force the powder and ball down the barrel of the musket with the ramrod. He made an easy target.

The musket was also inaccurate, especially when shot from farther than eighty yards. Few changes were made to muskets, however, until the 1800s. In 1814 revolutionary war veteran Colonel George Hanger wrote a book about guns called *To All Sportsmen.* Colonel Hanger writes about the musket used during the revolution:

Revolutionary war soldiers prepare for battle by loading their muskets and listening to battle plans.

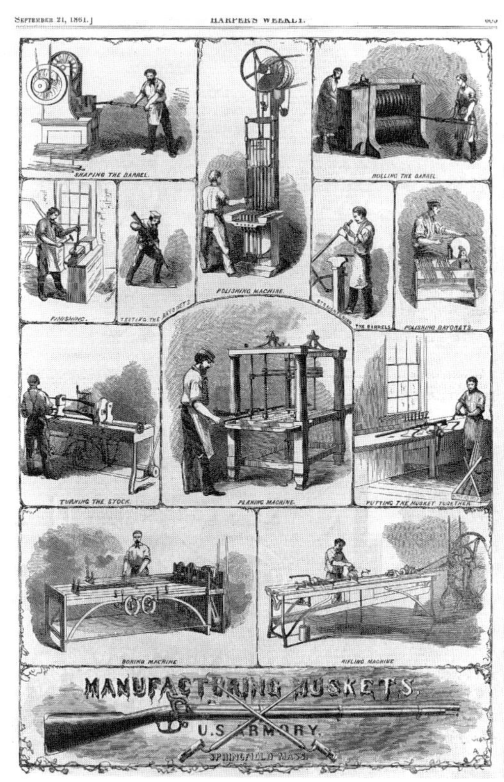

Two pages from Harper's Weekly *illustrate the manufacturing of muskets for the U.S. Army. Steps include filling cartridges, shaping the barrel, and rifling the barrel.*

> A soldier's musket, if not exceedingly ill-calibrated (and many of them are), will strike the human figure at 80 yards, but a soldier has to be most unfortunate to be wounded by a common musket at 150 yards, assuming his antagonist [foe] had aimed at him; and as for firing at a man from 200 yards, the odds against hitting the target are about as high as if you were to fire at the Moon.

This sentiment was common and pointed out the need for a more accurate gun.

Rifled Muskets

Soon after the American Revolution new immigrants arrived from Europe, bringing their firearms with them. One type of German gun, the rifled musket, was particularly popular with settlers.

The principle behind rifled muskets is as old as bows and arrows. Archers know that putting angled feathers on the ends of arrows make the arrows spin as they fly through the air. The spinning motion makes an arrow more stable as it flies. Arrows constructed this way fly farther and are more accurate than other types of arrows. During the 1500s gunmakers Gaspard Kollner of Austria and August Kotter of Germany adapted this principle to guns. They cut deep grooves in the barrel of smoothbore muskets. These grooves were called rifling, and the guns that were made this way were called rifled muskets, or rifles. Rifling the gun barrel

SMOOTHBORE AND RIFLED BARRELS

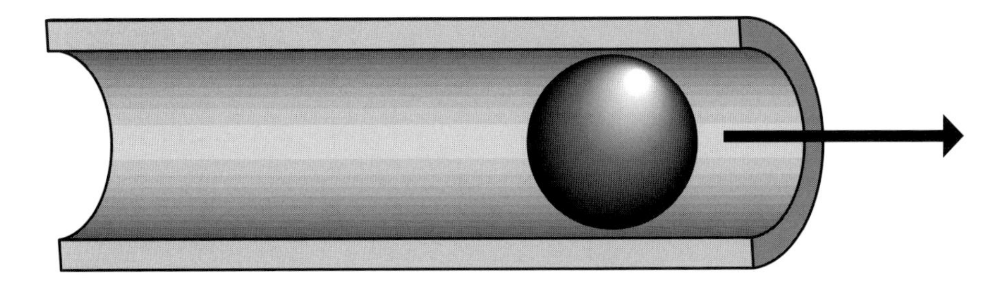

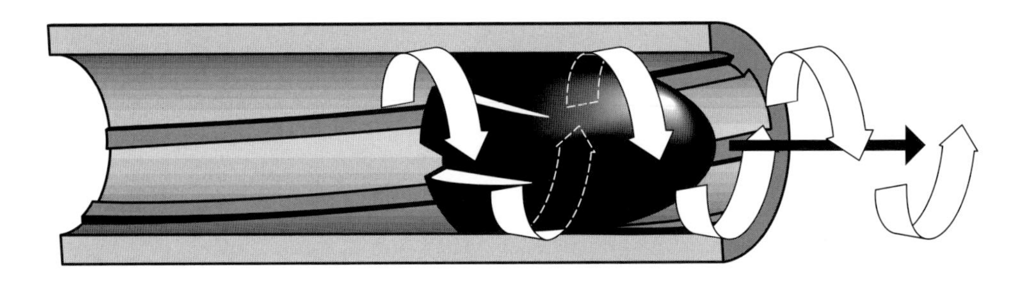

The barrels of the earliest guns were smooth inside so that a projectile, usually a round ball, could slide in and out easily. Since the barrel did not grip the ball in any manner, it did not impart any spin on the ball as it left the end of the barrel. In some ways it is curious that early gun makers did not attempt to make the ball spin because archers had known for centuries that a spinning arrow flies farther and straighter than an arrow that does not spin. A bullet behaves the same way as an arrow, because an object turning around an axis tends to be more stable as it moves through space than an object that is not spinning. This tendency is known as gyroscopic stability.

In the sixteenth century, gun makers accidentally discovered how to make use of gyroscopic stability. They began to carve spiral grooves, known as rifling, inside the barrel, probably to keep carbon deposits from building up on the surface of the barrel. As the ball followed the twisting grooves down the barrel, the ball began to turn. As a result, the ball left the barrel spinning. The spinning motion caused by rifling made the shot accurate at twice the distance achieved by smoothbore firearms.

made the bullet spin when it was fired, and this spinning action helped the bullets fly farther and straighter. Thus it was easier for the shooter to hit a target. But there were also many disadvantages to early rifles.

In order for the bullet to spin as it left the muzzle of the gun, it had to fit tightly inside the barrel. When rifling was first introduced there were only two ways to get a tight fit between the bullet and the barrel. If the bullet was the same size as the barrel of the gun, it had to be forced down the barrel with repeated blows from a heavy ramrod, or a ramrod and a mallet. The force needed to push a tight-fitting bullet down the barrel often broke the ramrods. If the bullet was smaller than the barrel, it was wrapped in a piece of greased leather or cloth to give it a snug fit against the grooves in the barrel. Either method slowed loading and made the first rifles impractical for battle.

European settlers counted their guns among the few cherished possessions they brought with them to the New World.

While the guns made by Kotter and Kollner in the fifteenth and sixteenth centuries were not well suited for the soldier, they were popular with European hunters and gamekeepers. They did not mind the extra time and trouble it took to reload, since the rifled musket was much more accurate than the smoothbore, or unrifled, muskets of the time. Over the years the rifled musket became the gun of choice for farmers, hunters, and anyone who depended on the accuracy of a gun to put dinner on the table. These guns were among the few cherished possessions the European settlers brought with them when they came to the New World.

The Kentucky Rifle

Pennsylvania, where many German and Swiss immigrants settled, was a wilderness rich in game at the end of the eighteenth century. Settlers found that they needed a gun that was not only accurate, but was also lighter to carry, had a longer range, and used less gunpowder. Gunpowder and lead were both hard to find in the wilderness. Some of the settlers had been gunsmiths in their homelands and were able to make quick modifications to their rifles to put them to better use in their new country. They narrowed the gun's bore so that smaller bullets requiring less lead could be used and less gunpowder would be needed for firing. The barrel was lengthened so that the gun would be more accurate over a longer distance.

Davy Crockett (far left) and Daniel Boone (left) were known as exceptional marksmen. Both used the Pennsylvania rifle, later known as the Kentucky rifle.

The entire gun was made lighter so that it could be carried for long distances without exhausting the hunter.

This modified rifle came to be known as the Pennsylvania rifle, and its reputation spread quickly to surrounding areas. By the late 1700s the Pennsylvania rifle had gained wide use among settlers moving west. Early frontiersmen Daniel Boone and Davy Crockett gained fame in Kentucky as exceptional marksmen. Their gun of choice was the Pennsylvania rifle, which had great range and accuracy.

Because of this rifle's popularity in the Kentucky wilderness, it came to be known as the Kentucky rifle. The Kentucky rifle had a reputation for accuracy at unheard of distances. An average marksman could hit a target the size of a man at 300 yards, while smoothbore muskets lost their effectiveness beyond 100 yards. In one demonstration a group of marksmen each put a bullet through a seven-inch target that was 250 yards away.

The Americans put the Kentucky rifle to great use against the British in the War of 1812. During the Battle of New Orleans, marksmen using the Kentucky rifle were hidden along the sheltering hills. Even with the additional time needed to reload their rifles, the marksmen took a terrible toll on the British

The Kentucky rifle's long barrel gave it great accuracy even at long distances. This rifle, built in 1817 by Nathan Kile, was fifty-eight inches long.

Americans relied on Kentucky rifles to soundly defeat the British in the Battle of New Orleans.

army. After the battle, the British had lost twenty-six hundred men, while the Americans lost only thirteen.

In spite of its amazing accuracy and range, the Kentucky rifle did not replace muskets as the standard firearm for the military for many years. Although the rifle had proved to be a more accurate weapon than the smoothbore musket, it was still much slower and required greater skill to load and fire than the average soldier possessed. The American military stood by its choice of smoothbore muskets for outfitting most of the troops in the War of 1812. Until the Civil War, smoothbore muskets dominated the battlefield.

The Minié Ball

While rifling the bore of the musket went a long way toward improving accuracy, a major change had to be made to the way a rifle was loaded or it would never become useful as a military weapon. In 1851 French Captain Claude Étienne Minié developed a new

Civil War soldiers pose with their rifles. Until the Civil War most soldiers used smoothbore muskets on the battlefield. But advances in rifle and bullet design made the rifle the deadliest weapon of the Civil War.

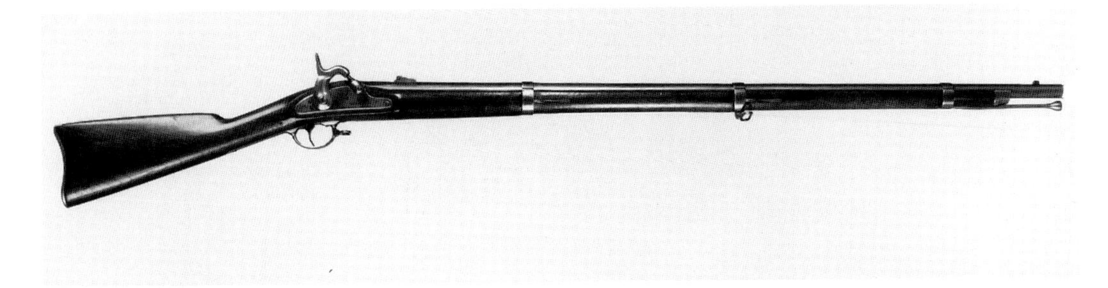

A rifled gun bore greatly improved accuracy. Shown above is an 1863 Springfield rifle.

type of bullet that made the rifle as quick and easy to load as a smoothbore. The bullet, called the minié ball, was similar in shape to a modern bullet, with a cone at the top and a tapered cylinder below. It was smaller than the bore of the gun so that it could be dropped quickly down the barrel into the powder, and the clumsy ramrod was not needed. The blunt nose of the cone was solid, but the cylinder was hollow. At the bottom of the cylinder was a small wedge, shaped like an upside-down bowl. When the powder below the wedge exploded, the wedge was pushed up into the hollow tapered cylinder, causing the soft lead sides of the bullet to bulge. The bulging bullet fit so snugly inside the barrel that it was forced to follow the spiral grooves along the bore. Once fired, the minié ball had the same range and accuracy of the older larger bullets, but none of the loading difficulties.

The minié ball dropped easily into the gun barrel, eliminating the need for a ramrod.

By 1855 the minié ball had been introduced to the American military, which promptly improved upon it. James H. Burton, the master gunsmith at the U.S. armory at Harpers Ferry, Virginia, found that a curved rather than flat cylinder interior would allow it to expand without the aid of a separate wedge. This was an important change because the wedge sometimes fell out of the bottom of the cylinder, making it useless. By eliminating the wedge Burton created a bullet that was more reliable and less expensive to manufacture than Minié's bullet.

U.S. gun manufacturers began at once to produce guns designed to take advantage of this new bullet. Many smoothbores were dismantled to have

Union and Confederate soldiers battle during the siege of Vicksburg. The use of rifled muskets resulted in a high number of Civil War casualties.

their bores rifled and quickly put back into service as rifled muskets. The country was by then on the verge of a civil war, and no one in the military had any doubts about the difference these new guns would make.

The rifled musket proved to be the deadliest weapon used in the Civil War. It was the most widely used gun by either side, with over 700,000 imported from Europe and the same number manufactured by the Union side alone. The rifled musket accounted for the largest percentage of Union and Confederate casualties. In the ten years the rifled musket was in service, during and after the Civil War, over 2 million were manufactured in the United States. The rifled musket was a good gun for its time, but that time did not last long. Shortly after the Civil War ended, the military found a gun even more to its liking.

Breechloaders

The gun that replaced the rifled musket was actually a reworked musket. Instead of loading from the muzzle, it loaded from the rear of the barrel, or breech. These guns were known as breechloaders. They were developed at the end of the Civil War by Erskine S. Allin, the

The Trapdoor Springfield loaded from the rear of the barrel, or breech. The trapdoor, or breechblock, through which the gun was loaded gave the gun its name.

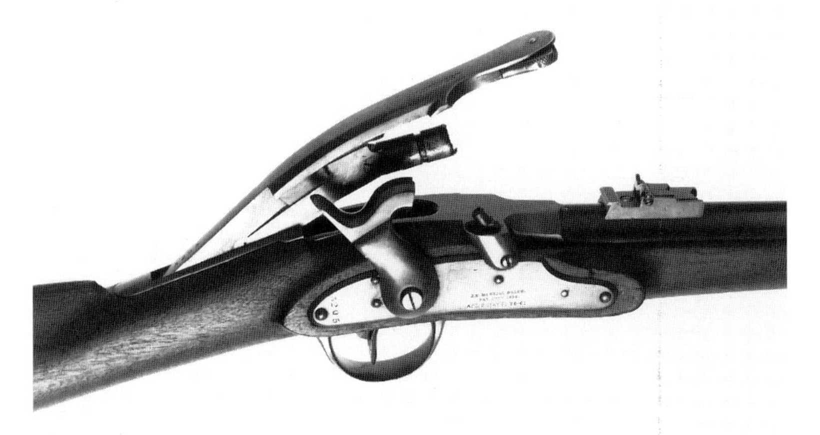

A close-up view shows the loading mechanism on an 1858 Merrill breech-loading rifle.

head of the Springfield armory in Massachusetts. Allin invented the breechloader from surplus military muskets. He called his breechloader the Trapdoor Springfield.

The Trapdoor Springfield's name comes from its loading mechanism, which resembled a trapdoor. This mechanism was called a breechblock. A hinge at one end allowed the breechblock to be flipped open between the breech and the stock so that the used gunpowder cartridge, containing the bullet and gunpowder, could be replaced with a fresh one. The breechblock was then closed to keep the powder from exploding back through the rear of the barrel, and the gun was ready to fire again. All this could be done in a few seconds, even with minimal training.

Eli Whitney, the inventor of the cotton gin, tried his hand at manufacturing breechloaders. He also introduced the idea of interchangeable parts and assembly line production at his factory in New Jersey. But Whitney's efforts were hampered by limited gun production facilities. Gun manufacturing in the late 1800s was dependent on water-powered machines or on handcrafting. The machining techniques available at the time could not produce the precision parts needed for safe and efficient use of the gun. This close, tight fit was important to prevent the exploding powder from flashing back through the breech and into the shooter's face.

Eli Whitney manufactured breechloaders, but his efforts were hindered by the poor machining techniques available at the time.

Potential buyers test their aim and accuracy at a mid-1800s breechloader demonstration in New York City.

Twenty years after Whitney's effort inventor John Hancock Hall solved some of the manufacturing problems. He was then able to set up assembly line production of completely interchangeable parts. Before this time each gun was made individually, and each part varied slightly in size or shape. It was difficult to find replacement parts when a part broke or wore out. With Hall's assembly line, however, one gun could be repaired with parts from another.

Hall's most popular invention was the Hall rifle because it boasted a unique feature. The stock of the rifle could be detached from the rest of the gun, leaving the owner with a powerful and easily hidden pistol. A pistol is a short gun that can be fired with only one hand.

The Hall rifle was the first widely used breechloader, but many others followed. Later breechloaders all had some sort of lever-action loading system in which the bullets were moved from a holder, called a magazine, located below the barrel. The bullets were positioned in front of the firing pin, which was the part of the gun that struck the priming powder.

The Sharps Rifle

The Sharps rifle was probably the best example of a refined breechloader. Invented by Christian Sharps, of the Harpers Ferry armory, the Sharps rifle was a great improvement on the existing breechloaders, which suffered from leaking gunpowder in their breeches. Sharps invented the drop block, a revo-

A Sharpshooter takes aim from his post. Union Sharpshooters had a reputation for deadly accuracy.

lutionary way to handle the problem of leaking gunpowder in the breech. The Sharps rifle had a small block in the breech of the gun that slid up or down in a slot, depending on whether the trigger guard was in place. When the trigger guard was lifted, the block slid to the down position, opening the breech for loading. When the trigger guard was snapped closed, the mechanism raised a small block up into the breech. This block sheared off the end of the newly inserted paper cartridge, exposing the powder in the end, while sealing off the end of the barrel closest to the breech. This sealing mechanism prevented leakage and backflash by blocking the end of the breech, thus protecting the shooter from injury.

The Sharps rifles were well respected by the military. So many requested them that the manufacturer even produced a special series of Sharpses just for the soldiers. It contained a mill in its stock for the soldiers to use to grind their morning coffee.

The Sharps gained a deadly reputation during the last half of the Civil War, when Union volunteer Hiram Berden formed a special company of soldiers trained in the use of the Sharps rifle. The company called itself Sharpshooters. Their skill provided crucial support to the Union army at Gettysburg. Berden's small corps, or group, drove back an entire regiment of Confederates. Using the Sharps, his men were able to fire nearly five shots a

Union volunteer Hiram Berden formed the group of specially trained soldiers called Sharpshooters.

minute, while the average infantryman in battle could fire only two.

The Sharpshooters were able to fire far beyond the expected range for an ordinary rifle. The typical rifle could hit a target at six hundred to eight hundred yards about half of the time. Using the Sharps rifle, Berden's men could consistently hit targets eight hundred to one thousand yards away, sometimes even farther. At one point during the war the men were told to drive away Confederate soldiers occupying an observation tower fifteen hundred yards away. A Union officer with binoculars climbed a hill near the Sharpshooters and waited for them to fire a round at the enemy. He then signaled to the men that the Confederates had looked down at the bullets striking the hill below them. The Sharpshooters adjusted their aim higher. Now the Confederates were seen looking up at the bullets whizzing above them. Another adjustment was made, and this time the bullets reached their targets.

The Percussion Cap

Loading improvements changed how quickly and safely a soldier could fire a gun. In 1805 a Scottish minister and amateur chemist, the Reverend Alexander John Forsyth found that a particular compound, mercury fulminate, would explode if struck sharply. Forsyth was an avid hunter and quickly saw a use for the mixture in improving the existing method for firing a gun.

Until this time mechanical firing mechanisms had all relied on a spark

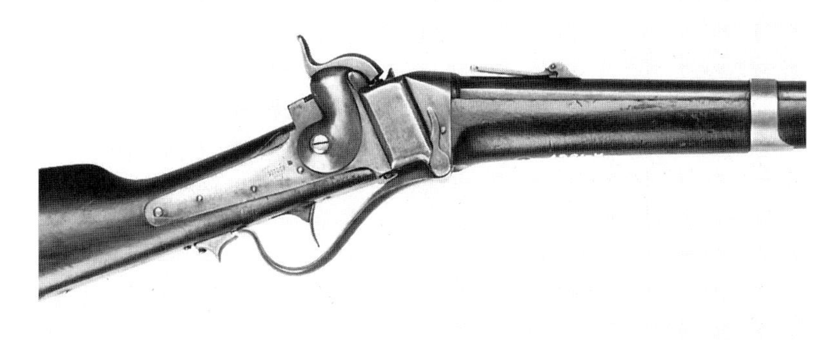

The Sharps rifle was highly valued by the U.S. military for its ease of use and its ability to fire over long distances.

PERCUSSION CAP

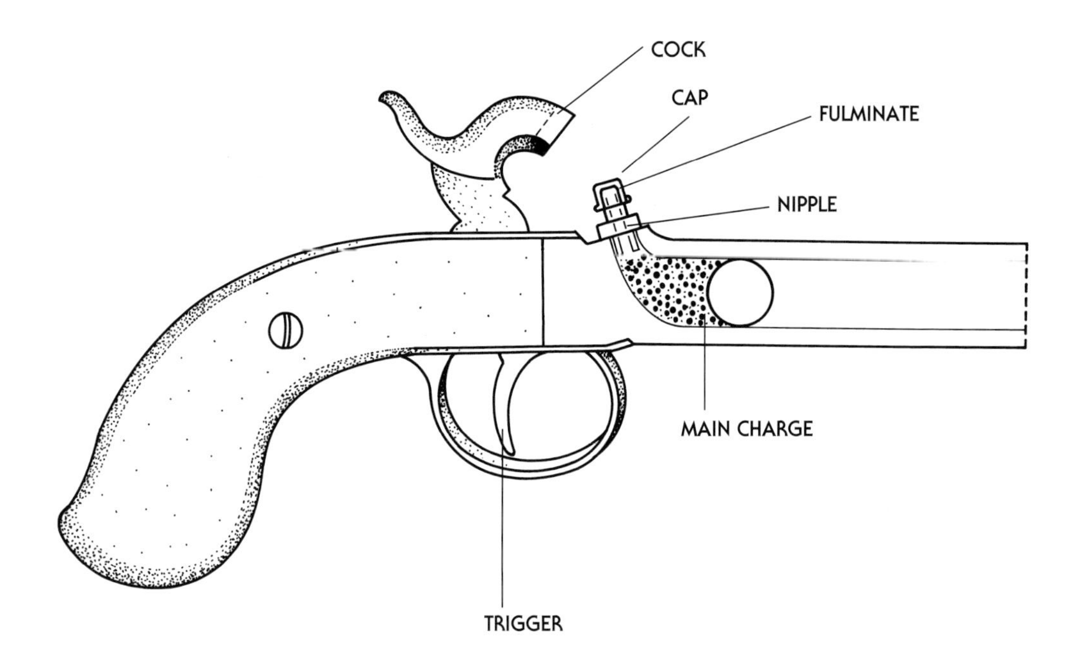

Like the flintlock, the percussion cap uses pressure from a spring-loaded cock to ignite the powder charge. But the percussion cap was more reliable than the early wheel locks and flintlocks because it was less vulnerable to problems created by wind and rain. Rain did not impede the functioning of the percussion cap because it did not rely on dry priming powder carried in a metal pan or open touchhole. Flintlocks also suffered from wind, which often blew away the sparks needed for ignition. This was not a problem for percussion caps since they did not require sparks for ignition.

The percussion cap took its name from a small, copper cap which rested atop a hollow, metal shaft, or nipple. The cap contains a highly explosive substance known as fulminate. When released by the trigger, the spring-loaded cock springs forward and strikes the cap. The force of the blow causes the fulminate to explode, sending a jet of fire down the nipple to the powder charge. This concentrated flame ignites the powder charge, causing the gun to fire.

being made by striking a flint or stone against steel. The spark then ignited the powder, and the gun fired. Forsyth proposed a change in the spark-striking step. He poured mercury fulminate, which he called "percussion powder," into the gun. The compound was contained in a small bottle attached to the side of the gun by a rotating bracket. When Forsyth tipped the bracket, a small amount of percussion powder poured from the bottle into the breech. Then the hammer was drawn back and released, striking the percussion powder. This created a spark which then ignited the gunpowder in the cartridge.

Forsyth's invention eliminated worries over the flint becoming too dull to strike a spark or falling apart from wear. Forsyth's bottle design also eliminated the problems of using loose gunpowder in a flash pan. Earlier it had been impossible to use a gun in rainy weather because the uncovered powder would not fire if it became wet or even damp. Moving the gunpowder inside the gun was also much less dangerous to the person firing the gun, since the spark produced by the percussion powder was inside the gun barrel and could not easily set off any other gunpowder nearby.

Forsyth patented his invention in 1807, but other inventors soon improved on it. Although many differently shaped containers such as tubes, pellets, and pills were tried, American inventor Joshua Shaw developed the best combination of percussion powder and container. Shaw molded a container that was shaped like a top hat from a thin piece of copper. He called his container a "percussion cap." The cap was placed in front of the gun's hammer on the tip of a hollow metal cone that extended into the breech of the gun. When the hammer hit the cap, the cone directed the spark down into the breech, igniting the gunpowder there. Shaw had found a way to make a gun that was truly weatherproof.

The percussion cap is considered to be the first step toward modern ammunition, where the priming powder that produces the spark, the gunpowder, and the shot or projectile are all contained in one cartridge. These cartridges would later make possible the multishot weapons that played such an important role in the American West.

CHAPTER 5

The American West

Countless books have been written and movies made about the cowboys, sheriffs, and outlaws of the old West. In these stories the villains rode into town with blazing revolvers only to be defeated by the sheriff and his trusty six-shooter. While much of this is simply Hollywood legend, the six-shooter, or revolver, played a major role in the American West.

Guns were a daily part of western life. Lawlessness prevailed in many towns and on the range. As Fred Lambert, the first marshal of Cimarron, New Mexico, recounted in his biography, shootings were a daily event in many western towns in the late 1800s. Citizens carried guns and used them often. The record for the number of men killed in Cimarron in one day was five, and Cimarron was not unique. Violence was a common occurrence in most western towns. This life-style demanded a new type of gun. The pepperbox pistol, introduced in the 1830s, was that gun.

Pepperboxes

The pepperbox pistol was a multishot gun, meaning it could be fired several times without reloading. The pepper-

Guns were an important part of life in the American West. Ordinary citizens carried guns and used them often.

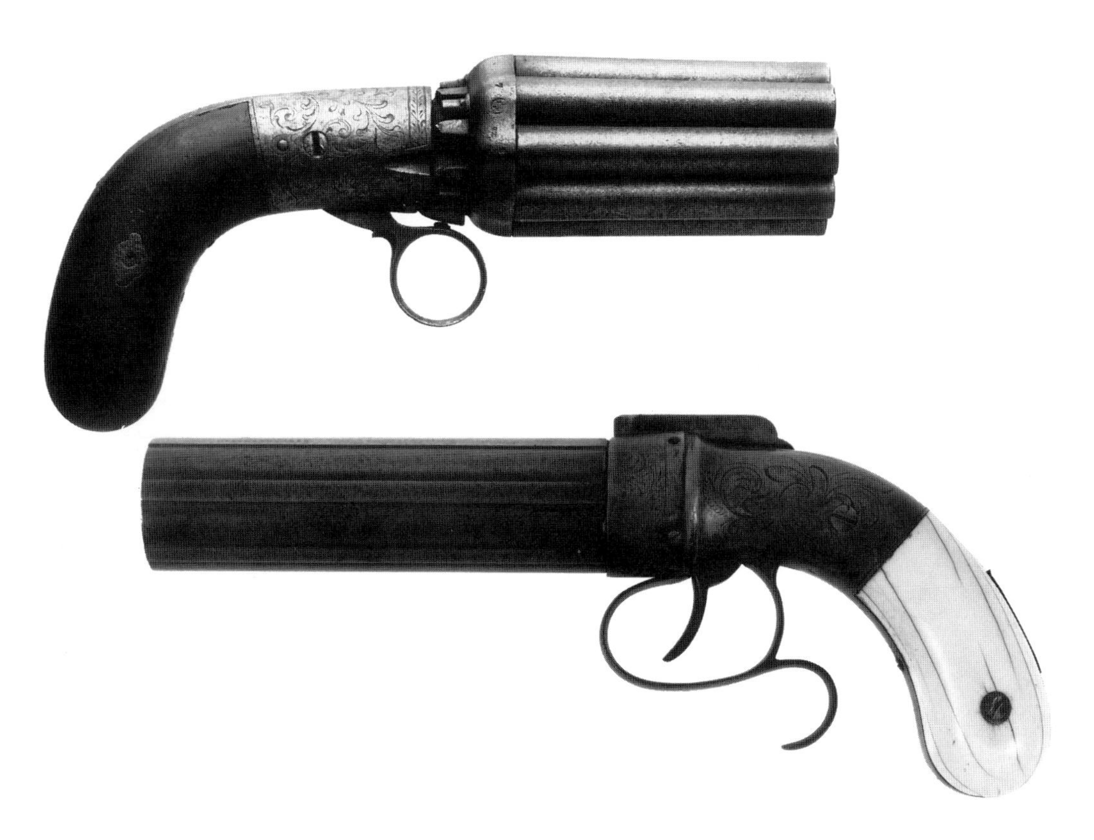

The Mariette pepperbox pistol (top) could be fired several times without reloading, although its multiple barrels had to be turned by hand. The barrels of the double-action pepperbox by Ethan Allen (bottom) revolved each time the trigger was pulled.

box consisted of a group of barrels bundled together. Each barrel held a bullet. The barrels were rotated by hand, as a unit, after each firing. A gunner could continue firing without reloading until the bullet in each barrel was expended. Most pepperboxes had four to six barrels, but at least one had eighteen.

Even turning the barrels by hand was faster than using the earlier, single-shot weapons, which required reloading after every firing. Inventors continued to look for ways to make the gun more efficient. In April 1836 brothers Benjamin and Barton Darling of Massachusetts received the first American patent for a pepperbox. Their pepperbox barrel revolved automatically when the hammer was cocked, eliminating the need for turning it by hand.

Within a year the pepperbox underwent another change, this one even more impressive than the last. In 1837 inventor Ethan Allen, also of Massachusetts, invented a double-action pepperbox. A single pull on the trigger revolved the barrels and fired the gun. The double-action pepperbox was the fastest firing gun ever seen up to that point. Like many other new inventions, it had drawbacks. Because the barrel turned while the gun fired, bullets often flew erratically. Also, gunners found the revolving barrel a distraction when they took aim.

Author Mark Twain captured the

essence of the pepperbox performance problems better than most when he wrote in 1861:

> To aim along the turning barrel and hit the thing aimed at was a feat which was probably never done with [a pepperbox] in the world. . . . If she [the gun] didn't get what she went after, she would fetch [hit] something else. . . . She went after a [two] of spades nailed against a tree, once, and fetched a mule standing about thirty yards to the left of it. [The gunman] did not want the mule; but the owner came out with a double-barreled shotgun and persuaded him to buy it anyhow. It was a cheerful weapon—the [pepperbox]. Sometimes all its six barrels would go off at once, and then there was no safe place in all the region roundabout but behind it.

The era of the pepperbox pistol was short-lived. But its contribution to gun development was long-term. The pepperbox no doubt provided the inspiration for the pistol that was invented in 1835 by a Connecticut inventor named Samuel Colt.

Inventor Samuel Colt developed a lightweight pistol that was easy to load and aim and more accurate than previous guns.

Revolvers

Colt's invention, called a revolver, changed pistols—hand-held guns—forever. Colt knew that using revolving barrels was a good way to have several shots available, but he could not find a way to overcome the problem of inaccurate aim. Instead, Colt designed a single-barrel gun with a revolving cylinder that held the spare bullets. When the hammer was cocked, the cylinder rotated, bringing the next bullet, or round, into firing position directly in line with the barrel. This not only made a repeating pistol that was easy to load and aim, but also one that was lighter in weight and, because the barrel did not rotate, much more accurate. Colt called his new gun a revolver because of its turning cylinder. It was also nicknamed a six-shooter.

While Colt's revolver would be recorded in history as the gun that won the West, at first he had little success with it. His first factory in Paterson, New Jersey, failed because he could not get enough orders for his gun. Colt tried to sell his revolvers to the military, but buyers in Washington, D.C., were not convinced that Colt's guns would stand up to the rugged demands of army life. They feared that the revolving cylinder would break and make the gun useless. Even though Colt could not convince government officials of his gun's abilities, military officers were impressed by its speed and accuracy. Many purchased the new weapon for their personal use.

THE COLT REVOLVER

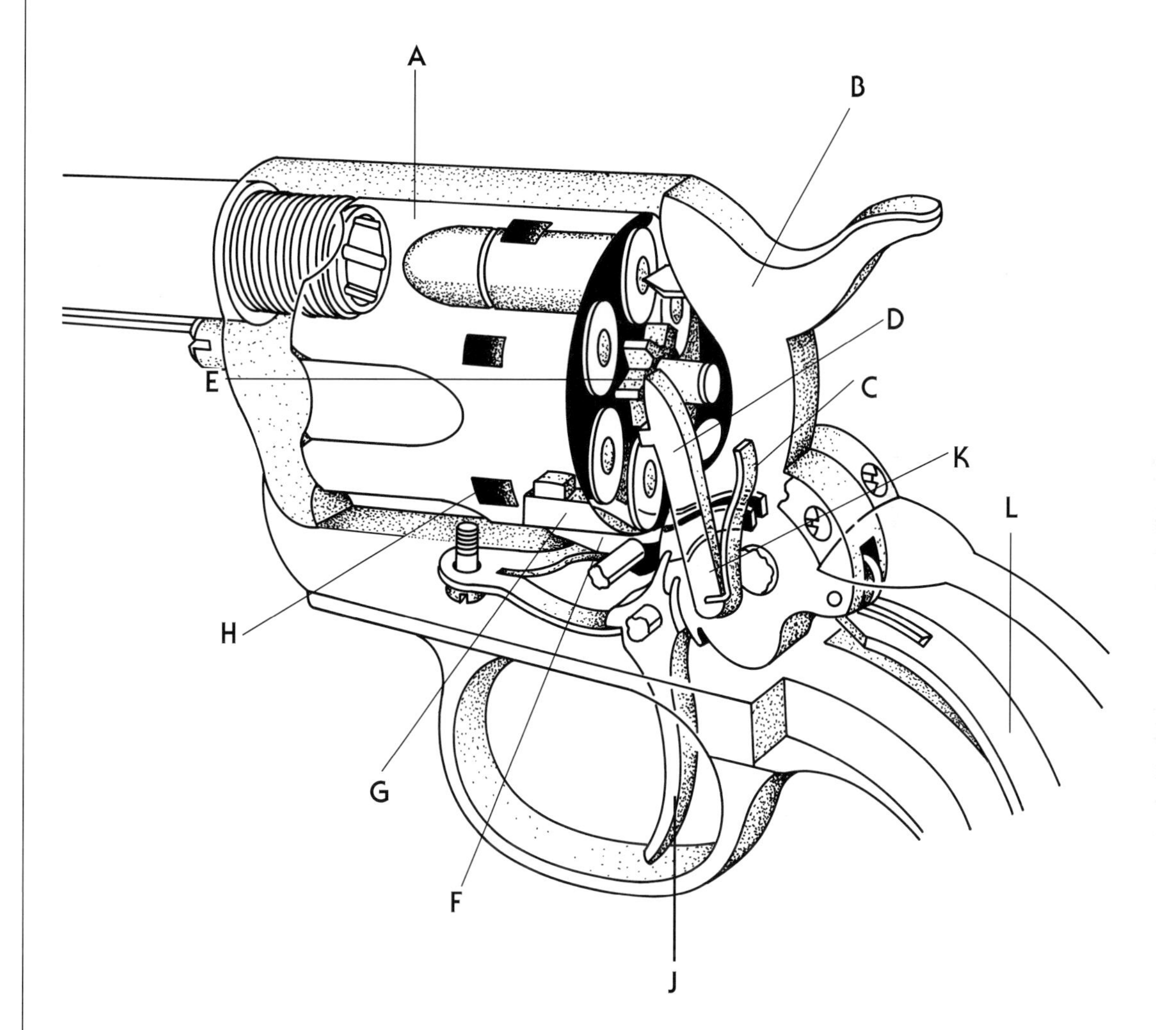

The Colt Frontier single-action revolver, first manufactured in 1873, has served as a model for all other breech-loading cartridge revolvers. With only minor changes it remains in production today.

The revolving chamber (A) holds six rounds, which can be fired in succession before reloading. The chamber revolves one sixth of a turn as the hammer (B) is drawn backward and a spring at the base of the hammer (C) lifts a metal rod known as the hand (D). As the hand rises, it presses against a small gear (E) fused to the chamber, causing the chamber to turn and bringing the next round into firing position. Pressure from the bolt spring (F) forces the bolt (G) into a recess in the chamber (H), locking the chamber in place. When the trigger (J) is pulled, it releases the cam (K) at the base of the hammer. Tension from the mainspring (L), turns the cam, driving the hammer forward until it strikes the round.

The Revolver Goes West

Some of these officers took the guns with them when they headed west to the frontier. It was here that the revolver made its mark on history. Colt's revolver was the perfect weapon for the western frontier. It was accurate, it could be fired rapidly, and its small size and light weight made it practical for use by someone on horseback.

These guns were perfect for the new Republic of Texas, whose lawmen frequently faced Mexican soldiers and Indian warriors. In 1839 Texas bought 180 revolvers, and many of them were given to the Texas Rangers, an elite fighting troop founded in 1823 to keep order and protect the Texas frontier. The rangers developed a reputation as tough and fearless fighters, as did many of the Indian groups they battled. The Comanche, in particular, were known as fearsome and skilled warriors. They could fire up to a dozen arrows for every shot or two fired from most guns. But even the skills and courage of the Comanche were no match for Texas Rangers armed with Colt revolvers. During one battle in 1844 fifteen rangers encountered eighty Comanche warriors. With the help of their revolvers the rangers killed forty-two Comanche warriors. On November 30, 1846, Captain Samuel Walker, one of the rangers involved in the fight, wrote to Colt about the pistols:

> The pistols which you made for [Texas] have been in use by the Rangers for three years, and I can say with confidence that it is the only good improvement [in guns] that I have seen. The Texans . . . have learned their value by practical experience, their confidence in them is unbounded, so much so they are willing to engage four

Although Colt could not convince the U.S. military to buy his revolver, many military officers bought it for their personal use. Its accuracy and light weight also impressed lawmen of the western frontier. Various models of the Colt revolver are shown here.

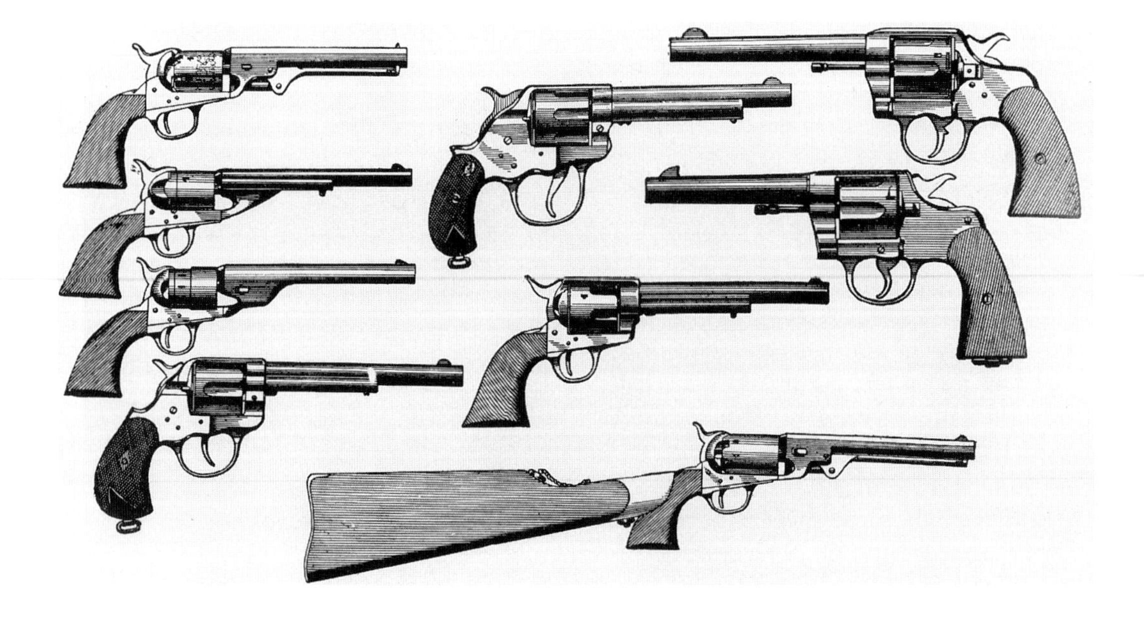

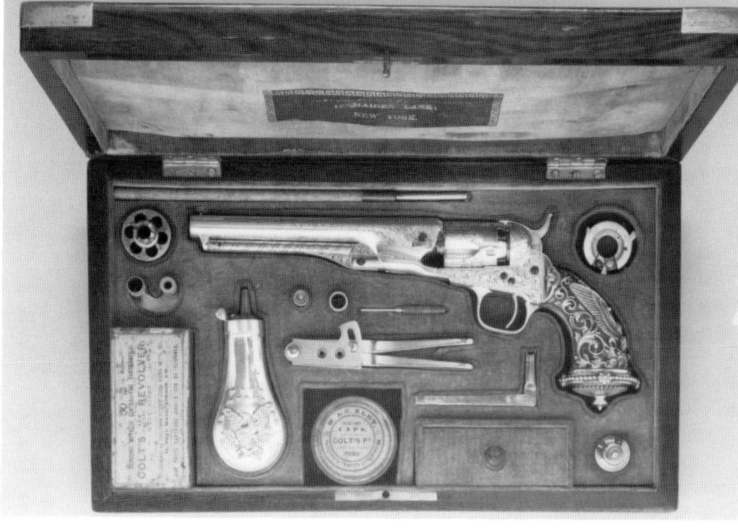

The Texas Rangers (above), an elite force responsible for protecting the Texas frontier, adopted the Colt revolver as one of their primary weapons. An 1862 Colt revolver and its accessories (left).

> times their number. . . . Up to this time these daring Indians had always supposed themselves superior to us, man to man, on horse. . . . The result of this engagement was such as to intimidate them and enable us to treat [negotiate] with them. . . . Without your pistols we would not have had the confidence to have undertaken such daring adventures.

Inspired by the ranger's glowing reports, the U.S. Army decided to buy the revolver for its troops. In a three-year period the military purchased four thousand Colt revolvers. Orders from outside the military grew too.

Among Colt's admirers was George Catlin, an artist who credited a Colt revolver with saving his life. During a hunting expedition in the western frontier, Catlin shot a buffalo with his rifle and failed to kill it. "Fortunately," he wrote, "I had one of Colt's revolvers with me. I drew it and turned and fired at his head. Instantly, to my great surprise and relief, he fell dead at my feet, the ball having passed through his skull and entered his brain."

News of the Colt revolver spread, and soldiers around the world wanted to own one of these deadly guns. In 1851 Colt showed his gun at the Great Exhibition in London and quickly attracted a flock of admirers. This inspired Colt to set up a factory in England. From England the gun's popularity continued to spread. There were reports of the revolver being used as far away as Africa, where English soldiers used it to fight against slave traders.

The Pocket Pistol

The revolver was not the only pistol to win a reputation in the Wild West. While the six-shooter helped bring order to the settlement towns of the West, another pistol gained fame in the cities of St. Louis and San Francisco. It was called the derringer.

The derringer was invented by a gun-making family from Richmond, Virginia. Henry Deringer learned his trade in his father's gun shop in the late 1790s. The family's workmanship was already well known. In 1806 the Deringers moved to Philadelphia and began producing weapons for the U.S. military. Between the War of 1812 and the close of the Mexican War in 1848, the Deringers built more than twenty thousand rifles for the federal government. It was during this time, in 1825, that Henry invented the gun that would make him famous. The derringer was a small but

Although small enough to be hidden in a pocket, the derringer packed a deadly force.

A defiant John Wilkes Booth shoots Abraham Lincoln in the head with a derringer pistol (above). The actual gun used to commit the crime is shown below.

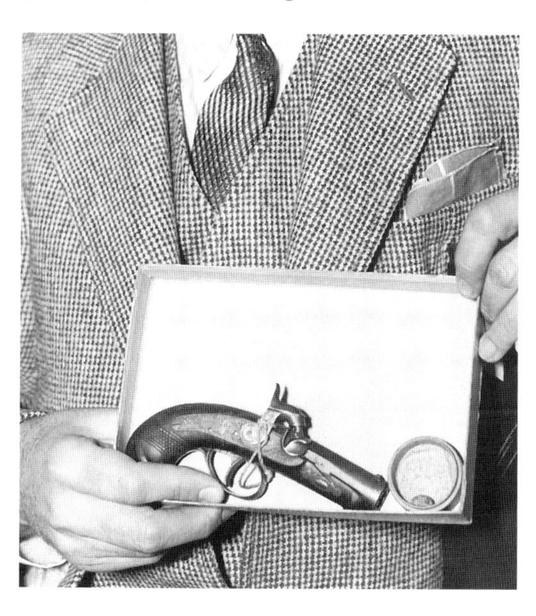

deadly gun that could be hidden in a pocket, purse, boot top, or woman's garter. It was the perfect backup weapon when one's revolver was taken away or when carrying a pistol was impractical.

The misspelling of the pistol's name began with the assassination of Abraham Lincoln on the evening of April 14, 1865. One newspaper reported that John Wilkes Booth had used a derringer pistol to kill the president. The misspelling stuck, and soon derringer became the accepted name for the pistol.

Even though the pistol's reputation was marred by the death of a president, the derringer quickly became popular.

As one gun dealer stated in 1868, "the reputation [of] Deringer['s] pistol is high. There is no other pistol of that character that I know; the public have sought after it." Another catalogue advertised that "the shooting power of these celebrated weapons is well known to nearly every . . . frontiersman. . . . Their deadly accuracy, make them most desirable for 'sure work [killing].'" When the weapons first went on sale in 1849, they were priced from $3.25 to $5.00. But during the California gold rush in the 1850s, Deringer was able to demand top prices for his popular pistols. Some sold in San Francisco for as much as $20.00.

Faster Fire

Derringers and revolvers evolved with time. Many models were replaced by newer and faster guns. Technological advancements made possible innovative guns that could fire in a continuous stream without reloading, signaling the arrival of the rapid-fire machine gun.

CHAPTER 6

Rapid-Fire Guns

Although guns have many uses—for example, for hunting, sport, protection, crime, and crime fighting—they have always remained, primarily, a tool of war. In that respect their development progressed rapidly in the decades leading up to and following the two world wars. It was, perhaps, inevitable that inventors and hobbyists would try to build on the multiple-shot capabilities of guns. This is basically what happened. Even as refinements on revolvers continued, a few inventors were laying the groundwork for automatic, multiple-shot, rapid-fire guns. These are the guns that would be used in a new era of warfare.

One of the first inventions in this direction came from a retired Belgian army officer who, in 1857, constructed a group of fifty rifle barrels, arranged like a pyramid, that could be fired in succession at a target. When operated by a competent gunner, all fifty of the barrels could be fired within thirty seconds. In addition to being fast the gun had a range of up to 1.2 miles.

At roughly the same time an Englishman by the name of Sir James Lillie was building a gun that combined the multibarrel system with a revolving chamber. Lillie's gun had two rows of barrels, one above the other, and each row had its own revolving chamber. At the end of each row was a handle. By turning the handle a gunner could fire each barrel, one at a time.

Another British invention was the Ager Coffee Mill, developed by Wilson Ager. This gun received its name be-

An early rapid-fire gun, the Ager Coffee Mill could fire one hundred rounds a minute. Its name came from its uncanny resemblance to a coffee grinder, or mill.

cause it had a canister-shaped dispenser, called a hopper, on top and a hand crank on the side, like a coffee mill. The hopper was loaded with paper cartridges, which fell into the barrel of the gun. When the hand crank was turned, it pushed a cartridge forward and locked it into place. After loading the cartridge, the crank released a hammer, which hit the percussion cap and fired. The empty cartridge was ejected from the gun, and the next cartridge was loaded in its place. This gun was able to fire one hundred rounds a minute.

These early efforts to build rapid-firing guns did not win the support of military leaders. Most could not believe that a gun barrel could withstand the heat and pressure caused by shooting so many bullets so quickly. In some cases they were right. The early rapid-fire guns also had various mechanical problems, and soldiers simply did not trust them. One observer described the Coffee Mill's reputation: "[It was] as likely to get out of order as a lady's watch [but] even if it were not subject to [breaking,] . . . soldiers do not like it . . . it is so foreign to the old, familiar action of battle."

The Gatling Gun

The first successful rapid-fire gun was built by a North Carolina inventor named Richard Gatling. Gatling's father was a successful inventor who had built one machine for planting cotton and another for thinning it. Gatling shared his father's gift for inventing, and in 1850 he began work on a hand-cranked machine gun. Gatling used Ager's method of loading, but unlike earlier rapid-fire guns, Gatling's gun had eight

Richard Gatling's hand-cranked rapid-fire gun was powerful and reliable.

barrels mounted in a ring. The barrels were revolved by gears, and each of the barrels was fitted with a hammer.

Gatling first demonstrated his gun in 1862 to O.P. Morton, the governor of Indiana. The United States was embroiled in the Civil War at the time, and Morton was convinced that Gatling's gun would be a powerful weapon. Morton was so impressed by Gatling's demonstration that on December 2, 1862, he wrote to the United States secretary of war, suggesting that the gun be purchased by the government:

> I have been present at several trials of [Gatling's] gun, and . . . am of the opinion that it is a valuable and useful arm. Dr. Gatling desires to bring it to the notice of your Department, with the view of having it introduced into the Service.

Gatling built a number of guns to demonstrate their reliability, but he was unable to sell his invention to the government. For Gatling it was a case of being in the wrong place at the wrong time. Fearing treachery by a native of the Confederate South, the government in the North was unwilling to buy Gatling's gun.

Gatling continued to improve his gun despite his inability to sell it. For example, he replaced the hopper with a rotating drum that loaded the cartridges. This made the gun faster to load and fire. After the Civil War ended, and hostilities between the North and South began to fade, the army tested Gatling's gun. A report of the gun trials made by Lieutenant I.W. Maclay stated: "Gatling's gun seems to possess all the good qualities claimed for it; it is therefore merely a question of whether such a piece would be of use in actual service." The U.S. Army officially adopted the Gatling gun on August 24, 1866. Other nations, including Austria, Russia, and Great Britain followed by ordering Gatling guns for their armies.

Maxim's Machine Gun

As the threat of war grew on the European continent during the early 1900s, however, Europe's greatest powers found a replacement for their hand-cranked Gatling guns. As soon as the technology allowed it, they equipped their armies with fully automatic, rapid-fire guns, more commonly known as machine guns. This change occurred with the help of H.S. Maxim, who was born in Maine in February 1840, the son of immigrants who had fled England and France in search of religious freedom. Maxim had little formal education, but he had an intense interest in

An illustration of an early Gatling gun. Here, it is mounted on wagon wheels for easy transport to the battlefield.

how things worked. This interest led him to apprentice with a carriage builder, a gaslight maker, and to work for a time at a mill. While at the mill, Maxim showed his talent for invention. The mill was overrun by mice, so Maxim invented a mousetrap that would reset itself each time it caught a mouse. Although the traps sold well, Maxim received little of the money, which went, instead, to the company hired to manufacture them.

Despite not being much of a businessman, Maxim had an eye for the needs of the future. While visiting Europe in 1881, Maxim saw signs of growing tension, instability, and war. He decided the time was right for work on a new gun. He spent three years working on a gun that would fire a continuous stream of bullets as long as its trigger was depressed. By 1884 Maxim had completed his gun. It relied on recoil pressure, or the forceful backward mo-

Gatling poses with one of his guns. Despite his initial hard luck selling his gun, the Gatling gun was eventually used by soldiers around the world.

The Maxim machine gun relied on a mechanical recoil action to reload after each shot.

tion caused by the force of the gun's discharge. This recoil action reloaded the gun after each shot.

Maxim's weapon was the first true machine gun because it relied totally on mechanical means for its rapid-firing capability. Its automatic-firing capability made the hand crank of the Gatling gun obsolete. Maxim's gun also topped the Gatling gun's speed. The machine gun could fire 666 rounds in one minute, making it the fastest automatic gun yet invented. The U.S. Army showed no interest in the weapon, but European governments, perhaps sensing the approach of war, expressed interest in Maxim's invention. The British government bought three of Maxim's guns, and Italy, Austria, and Germany quickly followed suit. After seeing a demonstration of the Maxim machine gun, the German leader, Kaiser Wilhelm, declared that "this is the gun, there is no other." Germany built its

A demonstration of the power and technique of the Maxim machine gun.

THE MAXIM MACHINE GUN

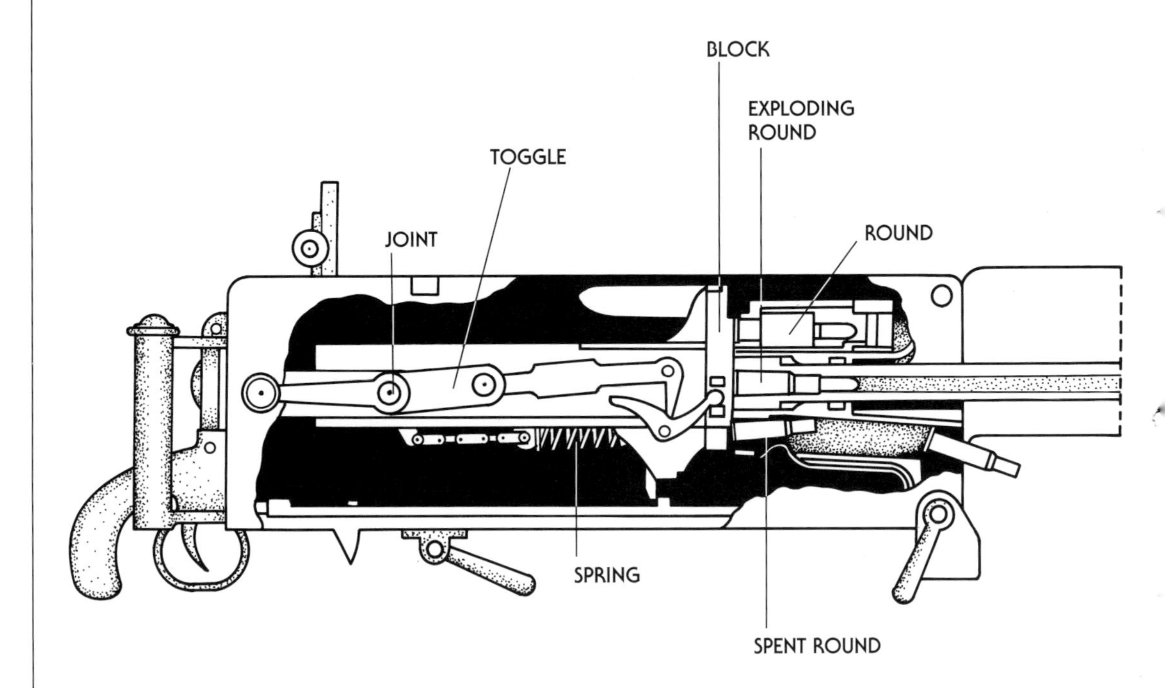

From his own shooting experience, Hiram Stephen Maxim knew that a powerful rifle creates a strong recoil when fired. In fact, more of the energy released by an exploding cartridge goes into the recoil than into propelling the bullet. Maxim realized that the energy of the recoil could be used to power the repeating action of a machine gun. By 1884, Maxim had harnessed this energy to power a gun capable of firing ten times a second.

When Maxim's gun was fired, the exploding round released much of its energy against a block. This pressure drove the block backward. The motion of the block caused a hinged rod, known as a toggle, to bend at the joint. As the toggle gave way, the block continued to move backward, tugging on the cloth belt that held the next round. This action drew the next round into the firing chamber and pushed the spent round out. After the toggle had flexed as far as possible, a spring drew the toggle forward once more. As the toggle straightened, it pushed the block back to the firing position and caused the next round to fire.

H.S. Maxim invented the Maxim machine gun after he sensed the approach of war during a trip to Europe in the late nineteenth century. His invention laid the groundwork for other rapid-fire guns.

own Maxim machine gun factory and by 1914 had produced fifty thousand guns.

Building a Better Rifle

Other rapid-fire guns were developed around the same time. One of these was invented by Ferdinand Mannlicher, an Austrian railway engineer. Mannlicher developed a repeating rifle that used a revolving cartridge holder to load cartridges. When the bolt was drawn back, a spring inside the magazine pushed a cartridge out of the magazine and into the firing chamber. Mannlicher's gun proved to be fast, efficient, and reliable. Greece, the Netherlands, Romania, Austria, and Italy all bought his gun as World War I approached.

While Mannlicher was building his gun, a German engineer named Peter Paul Mauser was developing a revolutionary rapid-fire rifle that would outshine Mannlicher's. The Mauser included an automatic cocking system, an improved locking system, and a superior cartridge ejection system. In Mauser's system, when the breech is opened, a mechanism cocks the firing pin, the cartridge is inserted, and the breech is closed, a process that makes firing the gun much faster. Mauser's gun also included a manual, or hand-operated, safety device. With this weapon there was no danger of accidental firing.

The first Mausers were produced in 1872. Like the machine guns, the Mauser proved to be an effective and deadly weapon. It was the first truly reliable and popular automatic weapon. It was simple to use and easy to care for, which made it ideal for soldiers during wartime. The Mauser design was so simple that there were no screws used to assemble it. A soldier could dismantle the gun for cleaning by using only the point of a bullet. In addition to being easy to care for, the gun was accurate at distances up to six hundred yards and was light and easy to carry.

Going to War

Machine guns, along with airplanes, tanks, and other sophisticated weapons of the modern age, transformed war. Hand-to-hand combat, once the staple of battle, became less frequent as warfare became more distant and impersonal than ever before. The world wit-

THE MAUSER BOLT ACTION REPEATING RIFLE

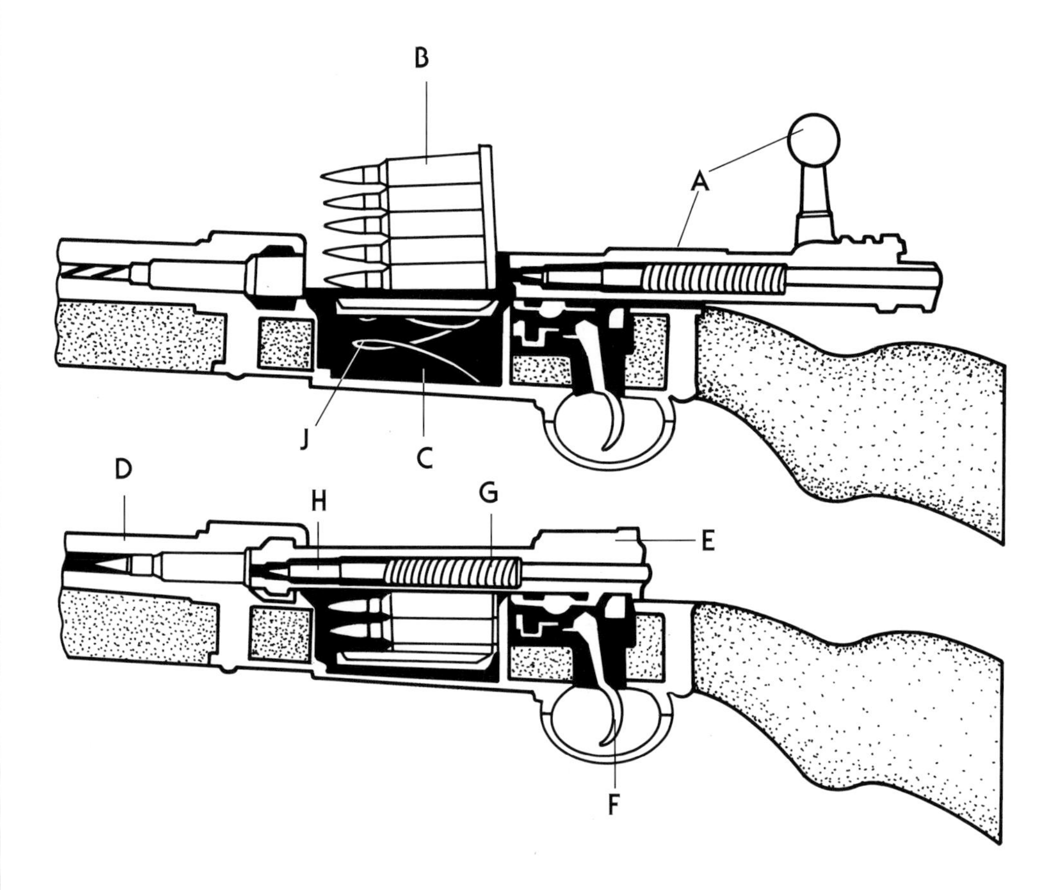

Peter Paul Mauser's solution to the problem of how to load a rifle both quickly and safely is known as the bolt action rifle. Mauser's design was the staple for military rifles for more than seventy years, and it remains popular in hunting and target shooting rifles today.

The first bolt action rifles were all single-shot, requiring the user to place each cartridge in the gun and remove the empty case by hand. Repeating rifles, like the Mauser, use a magazine with several rounds of ammunition and have a system of feeding the rounds one after another into the breech.

In the Mauser bolt action repeating rifle, loading is accomplished by lifting and pulling back the bolt (A) and inserting the bullet cartridges (B) into the magazine (C). When the user slides the bolt forward, one cartridge is pushed into the breech (D). The bolt is then lowered (E) and locked. The gun is now ready to fire.

To fire, the user squeezes the trigger (F). Pressure on the trigger releases the mainspring (G). The mainspring drives the firing pin (H) forward until it strikes the cartridge, causing the cartridge to fire. The rifle automatically reloads when the user lifts and pulls back the bolt, unlocking it from the breech. As the bolt retracts, it pops out the spent cartridge and a spring mechanism (J) pushes up the next round from the magazine.

nessed this transformation most clearly in World War I. Military historian Terence Albright said:

> The war changed the world's whole idea of what war was. In previous wars, battles were won by the side with the best sharpshooters, or the men who were better at hand-to-hand combat. The kinds of technology available in World War I, such as machine guns . . . ushered those days out forever. Wars became more impersonal. A soldier no longer had to look his enemy in the eye.

Historians estimate that machine guns inflicted more than 90 percent of all casualties in World War I. And there were many casualties in this war. In all, about 8.5 million people died during the war and another 21.2 million suffered injuries. The Mauser and other technological gains in weaponry in the years leading up to World War I made this conflict the bloodiest in history up to this point.

Postwar Efforts

Improvements in automatic weapons continued after World War I. American inventor John C. Garand began work on an automatic rifle in 1920, a project that took nine years to complete.

World War I American soldiers fire a machine gun during an Allied advance against the Germans (above), and French soldiers position themselves behind a machine gun ready to fire against German forces (left).

Garand's weapon was so effective that it was adopted as the standard service rifle by U.S. forces in 1936. Before Garand perfected this gun, American military leaders had resisted the idea of issuing automatic rifles and machine guns to all troops. They feared that soldiers would fire all of their ammunition in the first minutes of battle. They also thought that an automatic weapon would be too difficult for the average soldier to use and care for. But Garand's design was simple and his gun easy to use.

In the Garand gun a gas cylinder beneath the barrel fired the gun and helped it reload. When a shot was fired, gas was sucked out of the barrel through a tiny hole near the muzzle. The force of this gas exploding pushed the bolt back and ejected the gun shell. When the gun fired, a spring pulled the bolt forward again. This forward motion pulled the top bullet from the magazine and locked it into the firing chamber. As the bolt moved to the rear, it cocked the hammer. In this way the rifle loaded itself. All the gunner had to do was aim and press the trigger. When the magazine was empty, it was automatically ejected from the gun.

The Garand was one of the most popular guns of World War II. More than four million were used during the war. The only drawback to the weapon was its magazine-ejection system. When a magazine was empty, it was automatically ejected from the gun with great force. The empty clip flew often through the air for several feet before landing on the ground. If the container hit hard or frozen ground, it made a distinctive ringing sound. Anyone hearing this noise knew the gunner was out

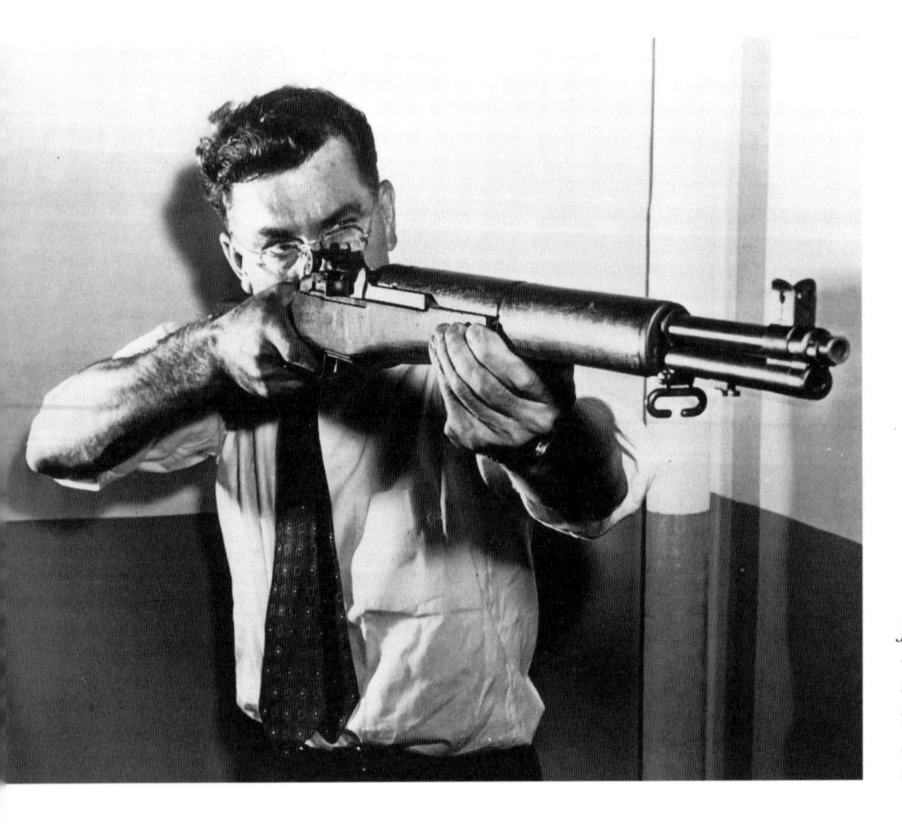

John C. Garand takes aim behind the automatic rifle he invented. The gun uses a gas cylinder to fire and reload.

Workers in a Garand gun factory prepare the rifles for shipping.

of ammunition and reloading his gun. An alert enemy soldier knew he could stand up and fire a few shots without fear of being shot at himself.

Submachine Guns

World War II also introduced the submachine gun to the battlefield. A submachine gun is a cross between a machine gun and an automatic rifle. It is smaller than other rapid-fire guns and so can be carried by hand and more easily concealed. The submachine gun is also fast and efficient. Some submachine guns could shoot from twenty-five to thirty-two bullets per minute, a rate faster than any previous small weapon. They were built first in Germany, but other countries also designed their own versions of the submachine gun. Most early models were crude, inspiring little confidence from German, British, and American military officials. But when World War II began in 1939, the British decided they would benefit from having submachine guns after all. They decided on the American-made Thompson submachine gun.

The Thompson had been invented two decades earlier by General John T.

An early model Thompson submachine gun. The Thompson could fire twenty bullets in less than a second.

Although the Thompson submachine gun was used in World War II (right), it is best known as the weapon of gangsters such as Al Capone (left).

Thompson. Thompson referred to the gun as a "broom to sweep the trenches." As a reserve brigadier general in the U.S. Ordnance Department, Thompson recognized the efficiency of the Maxim and another machine gun, the Browning, in World War I. However, he felt there was a need for a new kind of lighter, hand-held automatic gun and went to work on a new design. The first test guns were completed on November 11, 1918, the day World War I ended. Thompson's submachine gun could fire twenty bullets in less than a second with one squeeze of the trigger. Compared to later submachine guns, the Thompson was heavy, weighing 10.6 pounds, and expensive to make. But it was reliable, and many soldiers chose the Thompson even when there were other submachine guns available. Two million of these guns were used during World War II.

Despite its effectiveness in World War II, the Thompson submachine gun is better remembered as the weapon favored by Prohibition-era gangsters like Al Capone and the federal law enforcement agents who fought them. The tommy gun, as it came to be known, was often present at the scene of Chicago's deadliest shootouts.

Although it grew out of ideas from an earlier era, the automatic, rapid-fire gun made its mark during the world wars. Machine guns of all types are still used by the military today. They remain an important tool in the weapons arsenals of armies around the world.

■ ■ ■ ■ ■ ■ ■ ■ ■ ■ ■ CHAPTER 7

Antiaircraft Guns

World War II brought about a new type of menace—fast and deadly airplanes designed to strike deep behind enemy lines. To combat this airborne threat, military leaders needed a gun capable of firing shells far enough to reach these high-flying, fast-moving targets. Guns designed to shoot at airplanes are called antiaircraft guns. To build antiaircraft guns, inventors drew heavily on weapons developed during World War I.

Balloon Guns

World War I military commanders used hot-air balloons and crude aircraft to spy on enemy troops. The most direct response, and the only one that assured continued secrecy, was to shoot them down. This was no easy feat. Building guns to shoot at targets high above the ground posed a wide variety of problems. Among them was what to do about shells, which are the projectiles used in large guns, that failed to hit their target. Shells that were lobbed into the air fell straight down when they missed their target, putting the troops below at risk. Despite this risk, military commanders demanded that all enemy balloons be shot down. A 1910 military manual stated: "It has been [the objection] to balloon guns in general that our own troops will be endangered by the shells falling on their own heads. This objection is unsound. . . . A balloon . . . has to be destroyed by projectiles of some sort." Some of the shells aimed at the balloons weighed as much as twelve pounds, so they could do considerable damage when they fell on someone's head. The answer to this problem lay in self-destroying shells. If the shells did not strike a target within a certain number of seconds after leaving the gun, they would explode in the air.

Throughout the war engineers built guns designed to shoot down spy balloons and keep soldiers on the ground safe from falling shells. One German manufacturing company, Erhardt, built a gun designed to be mounted on a car so that gunners could chase the balloons and destroy them with rapid fire at short range. Another company named Krupp built a gun that fired an exploding shell that left a smoke trail behind it. The gunner could watch the trail and, if the first shell missed the balloon, could correct his aim based on the smoke trail.

Long-Range Guns

World War I also brought the development of long-range guns, which would provide another key piece of technology for antiaircraft guns. Long-range guns could shoot with great accuracy at targets miles away from the gunner. Gun manufacturers found that the larger the bore of the gun, the greater distance it could strike from. Larger-bore guns usually have longer ranges because their shells can be packed with more propellant. Because of the extra propellant, the shell travels faster and farther.

The German manufacturing firm, Krupp, based the design of its Paris gun on this principle. The Paris gun could launch a shell at such a high speed that it sped into the stratosphere, an area about seven miles above the earth. There, less affected by air resistance, the shell could travel long distances before it reentered the atmosphere to strike its target. During the planning stages engineers estimated that this gun would be able to hit targets up to sixty miles away. German leaders were enthusiastic and quickly set their manufacturers to work. While the gun was still in the initial stages, military leaders requested the gun's range be increased to seventy-five miles. Germany had targeted Paris for destruction, but its troops were still more than sixty miles away. To increase the gun's range, scientists rifled its barrel and developed shells that fit into the grooved barrel.

The Paris gun allowed German forces to bombard Paris from a distance of seventy-nine miles away from the city. The gun started firing on Paris on March 23, 1918, and the bombardment lasted 137 days. Altogether, 203 shells were fired into the city. At first no one believed that a gun could fire from this distance. As the *New York Times* wrote after the first days of bombing:

> [The] French capital is under fire. Ten have been killed and fifteen or more wounded in mysterious bombardment. . . . [that] puzzles Ordnance chiefs. No [gun] so far known . . . can cover such a range. . . . Officials at Washington doubt the 62 mile shelling; they say no gun could carry that far.

The gun rained destruction on the city and contributed to massive casual-

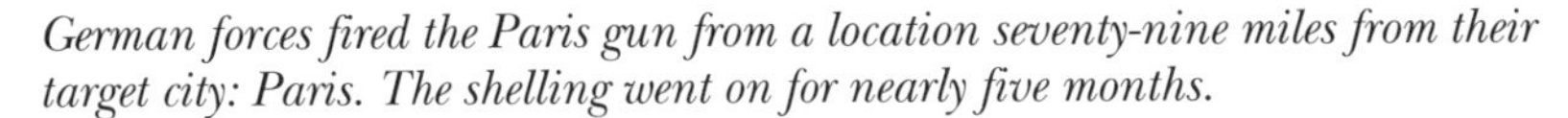

German forces fired the Paris gun from a location seventy-nine miles from their target city: Paris. The shelling went on for nearly five months.

ties during the war. The gun also proved that long-range weapons were possible and, along with balloon guns, laid the groundwork for antiaircraft guns that were to play a major role in World War II.

President Woodrow Wilson (second from right) and others stand at the site where the Paris gun had been fired one year earlier.

The Air Menace

Between the years of World War I and World War II, airplanes were perfected. They flew faster and higher and were deadlier than aircraft of any earlier era. To deal with this new airborne menace, inventors melded the technology of the balloon gun and the long-range gun to introduce a new type of weapon—the antiaircraft gun.

Germany was the first nation to build effective long-range antiaircraft guns. These guns could lob a thirty-five-pound shell to very high altitudes, making air raids over Germany a nightmare for Allied bomber pilots. The Allies lagged behind Germany in antiaircraft technology, but in 1940 the U.S. Army introduced plans for a 90-millimeter gun. By 1942 U.S. manufacturers were building two thousand of these guns a month. The 90-millimeter gun could be rotated 360 degrees to track planes across the skies, and it could be fired in an almost vertical position to shoot at planes directly overhead. This gun shot twenty-three-pound shells up to thirty-two thousand feet. The United States

U.S. soldiers fire an antiaircraft machine gun at a German observation plane during World War I. These guns had been greatly improved by World War II.

As the airplanes of World War II became more sophisticated so did antiaircraft guns. High-flying B-17 bombers pose a difficult target for antiaircraft gunners on the ground in Germany (above). Flight deck crew assists pilots and crew returning from a bombing run in 1942 (below). Not all aircraft escaped the sights of enemy antiaircraft guns.

also introduced the 120-millimeter stratosphere gun designed specifically to counter high-altitude German bombing raids. The stratosphere gun was able to shoot shells twelve miles vertically into the air.

The most famous antiaircraft gun used during World War II was the Swedish-made Bofors gun. This gun fired a two-pound shell at a rate of 120 rounds a minute. It was designed to be most effective in the seven thousand-foot range, an altitude at which most planes flew bombing missions during World War II. All Bofors shells had a self-destruct device that activated in the air seven seconds after it left the gun. This ensured that a shell did not injure ground troops if it missed its target.

Guns That Never Were

World War II also gave birth to a number of guns that never made it past the experimental stage. One of the most famous of these was the hypervelocity gun, which was modeled after the Paris gun, but designed to shoot at a much higher velocity, or speed. If this design

The Swedish-made Bofors antiaircraft gun fires two-pound shells at a rate of 120 rounds a minute.

had worked, the gun would have been able to shoot over a larger range than even the Paris gun. But trials with the gun found that the friction from the shell's speed ruined the gun barrel. During tests rifling on the barrel was worn away after only twenty-eight firings. This gun proved to be too impractical to use.

German forces experimented with even more fanciful guns. Allied troops found a weapon at the captured Hillersleben Experimental Range that they could not identify. It was made of an eight-foot cylinder with nozzles leading to its rear. After interrogating captured scientists, Allied soldiers learned that this strange device was called a vortex gun. Using a mixture of burning oxygen and hydrogen, the gun discharged a whirling vortex of air. German scientists claimed that the air could break a four-inch piece of wood at ranges of two hundred yards. The gun was designed to severely damage an aircraft, or at least create an air disturbance that would cause a pilot to lose control of the aircraft. But the gun proved not to be strong enough to damage an airplane or disorient a pilot, so it was never used.

The Magic Eye

Even though many guns did not work out, inventors continued to perfect the antiaircraft gun. One problem that plagued them throughout the war was targeting the moving plane. The main problem with airplanes was that they never stayed in the same position. Aircraft moved faster than any target before, and there was no way to predict if an airplane would fly up, down, right, or left to avoid a fast-moving projectile. The main problem, from the gunner's viewpoint, was that a gun shell took a

With the use of radar, gunners could calculate the location of enemy planes and plan their firing accordingly.

certain length of time to get to the aircraft, and by the time it arrived, the plane had moved. Gunners needed to know where the plane would be when the shell reached it. A new invention called radar offered the perfect solution to this problem. Radar was the magic cyc gunners needed to spot airplanes too far away for the eye to see.

The term *radar* began as a code name during World War II and is an acronym for *ra*dio *d*etecting *a*nd *r*anging. Radar is a device that locates objects by bouncing radio waves off them. By analyzing the radio wave a computer attached to the radar set can tell the distance, speed, and direction of a target. This was the information that aircraft gunners needed. Radar could "see" through fog and penetrate even the worst storms.

These radar systems replaced human calculation which was slow and open to error. New electrical devices collected data from the radar set and transmitted it continuously to a computer, which calculated the correct coordinates for firing the gun. The computer also made instantaneous corrections for wind and weather. When radar detection and direction systems were combined with electrical firing, antiaircraft guns became very efficient.

Radar control firing methods continued to be perfected following World War II. Radar targeting and antiaircraft firing have become so sophisticated that huge computers are now used to control them. These computers calculate target range, target distance and position relative to the gun, target altitude, wind strength, and type of ammunition being fired. In a few seconds the computer calculates all of this information and aims the weapon.

Over the years these systems have helped antiaircraft guns become "smarter" weapons, or those that can track and find their own targets. With the help of computers and radar sets, modern guns can seek out and destroy even jets that fly faster than the speed of sound—an idea that was unimagined during the days when antiaircraft guns were first created.

■ ■ ■ ■ ■ ■ ■ ■ ■ ■ ■ CHAPTER 8

The Future

If the history of gun development is any indication, guns of the future will be capable of firing bullets farther, faster, and more accurately than any before. During the next century guns will have new propellant systems and new projectiles, and they may not look anything like the weapons of today.

Faster Firing

Throughout the history of firearms gunmakers have been looking for ways to make guns shoot faster. Researchers have found that one way to increase a gun's firing rate, or the amount of time between one shot and the next, is to simplify the loading and chambering of the cartridge or bullet. Currently there are two designs being researched that would simplify this process. These are the cased-telescoped (CT) and Tround cartridge systems.

The proposed CT system would use a typical cylindrical cartridge, but in this cartridge the bullet is located farther back in the casing. It is surrounded by the gunpowder instead of being in front of the powder. This design shortens the cartridge, making the firing chambers and ammunition magazines smaller, and simplifies the loading mechanism. Instead of having to load a long cartridge with a tapered bullet at the tip, the gun has to deal only with a

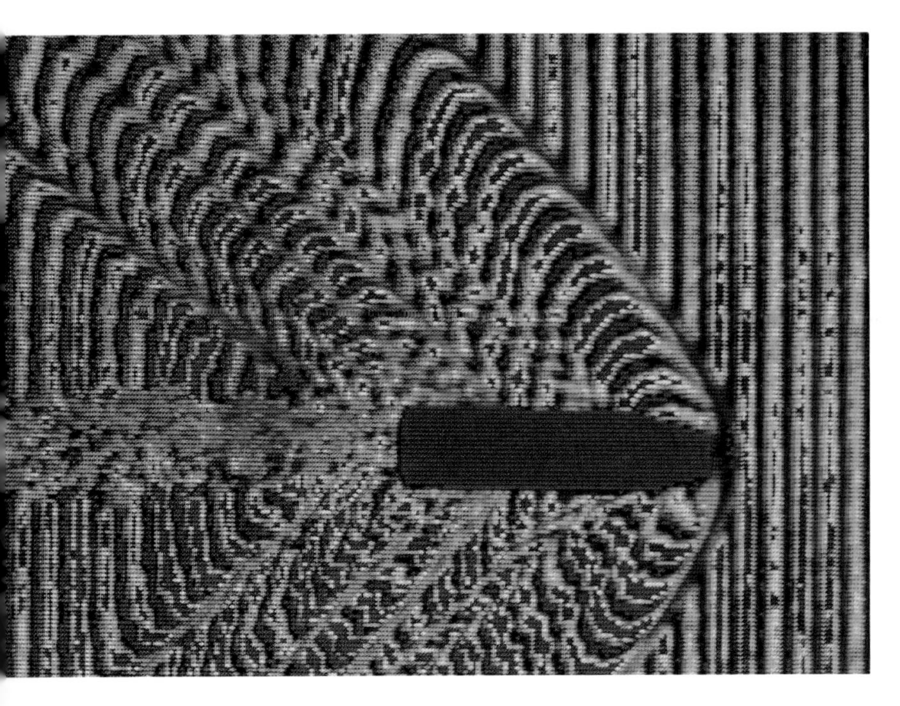

A high-speed, laser-enhanced image shows the pattern of air flow around a bullet flying at sixteen hundred feet per second. Reaching ever higher for greater speed, impact, and efficiency, researchers use computer and laser technology to design the bullets and shells of the future.

The electrothermal gun, which uses high-voltage electricity for firing, is designed to fire bullets equipped with target-tracking devices.

cylinder. This makes the loading easier and faster and gives the gunner a higher firing rate.

The Tround cartridge uses an idea similar to the CT system. The difference between the Tround and the CT systems is the shape of the cartridge casing. When viewed from the end, the Tround casing looks like a triangle with its edges slightly rounded. The advantage of this shape is that the loading and chambering mechanism can be simplified even more. The number of moving parts needed to load and fire a Tround is greatly reduced from the number needed for a traditional gun cartridge. Because its triangular shape is easier to grip than the usual rounded cartridge the Tround cartridge quickly moves into place once it enters the firing chamber. Both of these cartridge systems are being developed by the U.S. military.

In an effort to make guns fire faster, farther, and more accurately, scientists are also looking for new propellants to replace gunpowder. Researchers at the Los Alamos National Laboratory in New Mexico are working with a revolutionary gun design that uses high voltage electricity to fire a gun.

This weapon, called the electrothermal gun, is being designed to fire smart bullets, or bullets that are equipped with devices to track targets after firing. Smart bullets can lock onto a moving target and follow it as it changes course. The idea is to be able to fire bullets at a high rate of speed without subjecting them to the jolting and pressure that result from a gunpowder explosion. The sudden blast and jolting of gunpowder could destroy the delicate electronic devices used in the smart bullets.

The gun being developed at Los

Alamos will use four thousand volts of electricity to charge a thin graphite wire that is surrounded by a few tablespoons of water. The electric charge turns the water into steam, and the force of this pressurized steam shoots the bullet from the gun. This method fires the bullet with more force than can traditional gunpowder, but there is no explosion that could damage the smart bullet's electronic devices.

Another advantage of the electrothermal gun is that it fires bullets faster than possible with gunpowder. This higher velocity significantly increases the range of shots fired from an electrothermal gun over the range of a conventional gun of equal size. This is because the faster a bullet is traveling when it leaves the barrel of the gun, the farther it will go. In theory a relatively small electrothermal gun could reach targets at ranges of fifty miles. Small test versions of the gun have performed as expected, but full-scale models of the gun have not been perfected. Once this gun is perfected it could be used against missiles and aircraft and even used with special bullets that use sound waves to track submarines.

Researchers at the Lawrence Livermore National Laboratory in California are also beginning work on a new type of propellant. Scientists there are just beginning work on a light-gas gun that would use hydrogen heated to high temperatures instead of gunpowder to fire bullets. This type of weapon would be able to fire with unprecedented speed and force. In theory this type of gun could send an eleven-pound bullet hurtling through the air at speeds of up to 8,945 miles an hour. Some proponents of this type of system feel that larger guns could be built with this design to hurl rockets and satellites into space. But for now, the gun is still in the developmental stage.

Smarter Weapons

Guns of the future will have built-in devices to detect and track targets. One of the newest of these systems is the PHALANX close-in weapon system designed to shoot at fast-moving targets up to a mile away. PHALANX is a rapid-fire, twenty-millimeter gun equipped with a computer-controlled firing system and a radar set. The computer and radar systems allow the gun to search for, detect, track, and automatically fire

The PHALANX uses a built-in computer system to detect and automatically fire at targets.

Many U.S. naval ships are equipped with the PHALANX gun as protection against missile and airplane attacks.

at targets. The computer inside the gun can also determine if a target has been destroyed and will automatically cease firing once a target is eliminated. Early versions of this gun are being used to protect U.S. naval ships against missile and airplane attacks. The versatile gun also can be used against surface targets, like other ships, at short range.

Development of the PHALANX gun began in 1967 as a result of the sinking of the Israeli ship *Eilat* by a missile. After this incident the U.S. Navy decided there was a need for a new type of gun that could protect ships from the threat of missile attacks. In 1968 an American company named General Dynamics Corporation contracted to build the PHALANX gun for the navy.

Automatic Targeting and Firing

The PHALANX system is extremely accurate because it is able to continuously track and target an object while firing. It automatically directs a stream of bullets at its target throughout the firing period until the target is destroyed. Bullets from the PHALANX are fired by a modified Gatling gun that can fire forty-five hundred rounds per minute. The gun consists of a rotating cluster of six barrels that are loaded by a conveyor system in the gun. After each round is fired, the empty cartridge is automatically extracted from the breech and conveyed to the rear of the magazine. The gun is loaded with special ammunition designed to penetrate ships and missiles. Even though the PHALANX is already in use on naval ships, the government is still researching ways to make the gun faster and deadlier.

Into the Next Century

Chemically powered laser guns are also being discussed by scientists. These guns could be used for both land and sea warfare. They would shoot laser rays to burn incoming missiles and rockets from the sky. With a radar-guided tracking system, this type of gun could also be effectively used as an antiaircraft gun. Smaller laser pistols also have been discussed for use by the infantry. This type of pistol would use high-capacity batteries to store energy needed for the gun, which would fire short pulses of laser energy. While laser guns are effective in theory, there are a number of problems that scientists will have to overcome to make the guns a reality. These problems include the high amount of careful maintenance lasers require, the large amount of energy they need for firing, and the weather conditions required for a laser to be effective.

Some researchers predict that in the next fifty years guns may be built to fire hyperexplosive bullets—bullets that explode with great force when they hit a target. In theory these bullets would be ten times more powerful than those used today. Hyperexplosive bullets could be part of a rocket-assisted gun or fired from conventional large guns, but they would be given added range by a small rocket built into the bullet cartridge.

Century by century, guns have become more accurate, more efficient, and more deadly. Since the first crude firearms appeared about six hundred years ago, they have evolved into sleek modern weapons that can load faster, shoot farther, and hit harder and more accurately than the first inventors ever imagined. Even the most modern guns of today may soon become obsolete as new technology develops. But whatever the shape of the guns of tomorrow, they will continue to have a tremendous impact on our world.

Glossary

automatic: A gun in which continuous pressure on the trigger causes uninterrupted fire of numerous bullets.

barrel: The discharging tube of a gun.

bore: The interior of the gun barrel.

breech: Rear of the barrel, where the charge is placed.

breechblock: The part of a breech-loading gun that closes the breech.

breechloader: A firearm that loads from the rear, as opposed to weapons that load from the mouth of the barrel.

caliber: The diameter of the bore of the barrel.

cartridge: Contains the priming powder, explosive charge, and bullet in a single case.

chamber: The part of the breech where the charge or cartridge is placed.

flash pan: A concave piece of metal set into the barrel of a gun that holds priming powder.

gunpowder: A chemical compound that is used as a propellant in guns.

magazine: The metal container that holds the cartridges of a repeating gun.

musket: A heavy, long-barreled smoothbore shoulder gun.

muzzle: The mouth of the barrel.

pistol: A small firearm made to be held and fired with one hand.

priming powder: A small amount of gunpowder that is used to ignite the propellant powder inside of the gun.

propellant charge: Gunpowder placed behind the bullet. When the propellant is ignited by priming powder it causes the bullet to shoot down the barrel of the gun.

ramrod: A metal stick used to push a charge into a muzzle-loading gun.

recoil: The kickback, or backward motion, caused by the firing of a gun.

repeater: A gun that allows several shots to fire without reloading the weapon.

revolver: A gun with a revolving cylinder that holds numerous cartridges.

rifle: A gun with spiral grooves cut into the inside of the barrel to increase accuracy.

smoothbore: Having no grooves or ridges on the inner surface of the barrel.

stock: The part of the gun that holds the firing mechanism and the barrel of the gun.

For Further Reading

John Batchelor and John Walter, *Handgun: From Matchlock to Laser-Sighted Weapon.* New York: Talos Books, 1988.

A.J.R. Cormack, *The World Encyclopedia of Modern Guns.* London: Octopus Books, 1979.

Ian Hogg, *An Illustrated History of Firearms.* London: Quarto Publishing, 1980.

Andrew Kershaw and Ian Close, eds., *Weapons and War Machines.* New York: Crescent Books, 1975.

Harold L. Peterson, *Pageant of the Gun.* New York: Doubleday & Company, 1967.

Works Consulted

M.L. Brown, *Firearms in Colonial America.* Washington, DC: Smithsonian Institution Press, 1980.

David Butler, *United States Firearms: The First Century.* New York: Winchester Press, 1971.

William Edwards, *Civil War Guns,* Harrisburg, PA: The Stackpole Company, 1962.

W.W. Greener, *The Gun and Its Development.* New York: Bonanza Books, 1910.

Robert Held, *The Age of Firearms.* New York: Harper & Brothers, 1957.

Major F.W.A. Hobart, *Pictorial History of the Machine Gun.* New York: Drake Publishers, 1972.

Curt Johnson, *Artillery.* London: Octopus Books, 1975.

Sergio Masini and Gian Rodolfo Rotasso, *Complete Book of Firearms.* New York: Portland House, 1988.

Michael Newton, *Armed and Dangerous.* Cincinnati: Writer's Digest Books, 1990.

Major Hugh Bertie Campbell Pollard, *A History of Firearms.* New York: Lenox Hill Publishing, 1973.

L.R. Wallack, *The Anatomy of Firearms,* New York: Simon and Schuster, 1965.

Index

Ager, Wilson, 63
Ager Coffee Mill, 63-64
airplanes, 75, 77, 79-81
Albright, Terence, 71
Allen, Ethan, 55
Allin, Erskine S., 47
American revolutionary war, 40-41
American West, 54, 58-59, 62
ammunition, 20, 53, 82-83
antiaircraft guns, 75-81
  Bofors gun, 78-79
  90-millimeter gun, 77
  120-millimeter stratosphere gun, 78
antimissile guns, 84-86
arrows, 41
artillerymen, 34

backflash, 50
Bacon, Roger, 13-15
balloon guns, 75
barrel, 20
  rifling of, 41-44
  smoothbore, 42-43, 46
Battle of Crécy, 16
Battle of Gettysburg, 50
Battle of New Orleans, 44
Belli, Piernio, 33
Berden, Hiram, 50
black powder, 13-17
  as black magic, 13
  explosion of, 15-16
  ingredients of, 13
  use in war, 16-17
  see also gunpowder
Bofors gun, 78-79
Boone, Daniel, 44
Booth, John Wilkes, 61
Bourgeoy, Marin le, 29
breechloaders, 47-50
bullets, 32, 43.
  hyperexplosive, 86
  lead, 43
  minié ball, 46
  smart bullets, 83-84
  see also shells; shot
Burr, Aaron, 39,
Burton, James H., 46

cartridge, 48, 50, 53, 82-83
  paper, 30-31, 50
  Tround, 83
Catlin, George, 59
charcoal, 13
Charles I (king of England), 40
Civil War (U.S.), 45, 47, 50, 64-65
Clemens, Samuel, 55
Colt, Samuel, 56-60
Comanche Indians, 58-59
computer-controlled guns, 84-86
computers, 80-81
Crockett, Davy, 44
crossbow, 12

Darling, Barton, 55
Darling, Benjamin, 55
da Vinci, Leonardo, 23-24
Deringer, Henry, 60, 62
derringer pistol, 60-62
Dickinson, Charles, 38-39
drop block (breechblock), 49-50
dueling, 38-39

electrothermal gun, 83-84
explosives, 16

firearms. *see* guns
fire tube, 16-17
fireworks, 12
  in China, 13
firing device, mechanical, 20, 51-53
  Ager Coffee Mill, 64
  breechblock, 48

drop block, 50
flintlock, 27-29
invented by clockmakers, 25
machine gun, 67-68
matchlock, 20-22
Mauser bolt action rifle, 69-70
snaphaunce, 26
Spanish matchlock, 27, 29
wheel lock, 23-26
firing system
cased-telescoped (CT), 82-83
computer-controlled, 84-86
PHALANX, 86
radar targeted, 80-81, 84-86
Tround cartridge, 83
flint, 25, 27-28, 53
flintlock muskets, 27-30
use in war, 30-31
Forsyth, Rev. Alexander John, 51, 53

Garand, John C., 71-72
Garand automatic rifle, 71-72
use in war, 72
Gatling, Richard, 64-65
Gatling gun, 64-65, 85-86
General Dynamics Corporation, 85
Gheyn, Jacob de, 36-37
gun control laws, 35, 38
gun manufacturing, 46-49, 56
assembly line production, 49
Colt pistol in England, 60
Erhardt, 75
Krupp, 75-76
gunpowder, 20, 22, 24, 36-37, 43, 53
fireworks and, 12
replaced by electricity, 83-84
replaced by gas, 84
see also black powder
guns, 19
accuracy of, 40-45, 51, 56, 85-86
antiaircraft, 75-81
antimissile, 84-86
balloon, 75
computer-controlled, 84-86
craftsmanship, 26
double-action, 55
dueling, 38-39
firing action and parts
Ager Coffee Mill, 64
breechloaders, 48
fire tubes, 16
flintlock, 28-29
Garand automatic rifle, 72
hand cannons, 18
machine gun, 67-68
Mannlicher repeating rifle, 69
matchlock musket, 20-22
Mauser bolt action rifle, 69-70
minié ball, 46
pepperbox pistol, 55
percussion cap, 52-53
revolver, 56-57
serpentine, 22
Sharps rifle, 50
snaphounce, 27
Spanish lock, 27
wheel lock, 24-25
gun control laws, 35, 38
history of, 12, 19-31
hunting and, 35, 43
long-range, 75-77
machine, 65, 71
multishot, 54, 63
rapid-fire, 63-74
reckless use of, 35, 38, 54
safety device, 69
single-action, 57
use in war, 32-34, 44-45, 47, 50-51, 69, 71-78
guns, experimental
cased-telescoped, 82-83
electrothermal, 83-84

hypervelocity, 78-79
laser, 86
light-gas, 84
Tround cartridge, 83
vortex, 79
Gustav Adolph II (king of Sweden), 30-31
gyroscopic stability, 42

Hall, John Hancock, 49
Hamilton, Alexander, 39
hand cannons, 18-20
Hanger, George, 40
Henry VII (king of England), 35
Henry VIII (king of England), 35
hypervelocity gun, 78-79

Jackson, Andrew, 38-39
James II (king of Scotland), 23

Kaiser Wilhelm, 67
Kentucky rifle, 44-45
knights, 32-34
Kollner, Gaspard, 41, 43
Kotter, August, 41, 43

Lambert, Fred, 54
laser guns, 86
Lawrence Livermore National Laboratory, 84
light-gas gun, 84
Lillie, Sir James, 63
Lincoln, Abraham, 61
Los Alamos National Laboratory, 83-84
Louis XIV (king of France), 29

machine guns, 65
Thompson sub-machine guns, 73-74
use in war, 69, 71-74
Maclay, I.W., 65
Management of Arms, Arquebuses, Muskets, and Pikes, The, 36-37
Mannlicher, Ferdinand, 69
marksmen, 44. *See* Sharpshooters
matchlock, 20-22
Mauser, Peter Paul, 69
Maxim, Hiram Stephen, 65-66, 69
mercenaries, 34
mercury fulminate, 51-53
Minié, Claude Étienne, 45
minié ball, 46
Morton, O.P., 64
musketeer, 36-37
muskets, 20-31, 40
breechloaders, 47-50
flintlock, 27-30
matchlock, 20-23, 36-37
rifled, 41, 47
Spanish matchlock, 27, 29
use in war, 22-23, 26-27, 30-31, 40-41, 45
wheel lock, 23-26

paper cartridge, 30-31, 50
Paris gun, 76-77
peasants as soldiers, 34, 40
Pennsylvania rifle, 44
pepperbox pistol, 54-56
percussion cap, 52-53
percussion powder, 53
PHALANX weapon system, 84-86
pistol, 49
Colt revolver, 56-60
derringer, 60-62
pepperbox, 54-56
pocket, 60
poaching, 35
priming powder, 22
pyrite, 24

radar, 80-81
ramrod, 20, 40, 43, 46
rapid-fire guns, 63-74
recoil pressure, 66-68

revolver, 56-60
rifled musket, 41, 47
rifles, 41
  Garand automatic, 71-72
  Hall, 49
  Kentucky, 44-45
  Mannlicher repeating, 69
  Mauser bolt action, 69-70
  Pennsylvania, 44
  Sharps, 49-51
  use in war, 44-45, 50, 69, 72
rifling (barrel), 41-43

saltpeter (salt crystals), 13
schappahn, 27
Schwarz, Berthold, 15-16
Scott, Robert, 31
Sharps, Christian, 49
Sharpshooters, 50-51
Sharps rifle, 49-51
  use in war, 50
Shaw, Joshua, 53
shells, 75-77
shot, 20, 22. *See* bullets
six-shooter. *See* revolver
slow match, 18-19, 21-23
  replaced by friction, 25
snaphounce, 26-27
Spanish matchlock, 27, 29
sulphur, 13
surgery, bullet wounds, 32

Texas Rangers, 58-59
Thompson, John T., 73-74
Thompson sub-machine gun, 73-74
To All Sportsmen, 40
tommy gun (Thompson sub-machine gun), 74
touch hole, 16, 18-19
Trapdoor Springfield, 48
Treatise on War and the Military, 33
trigger, 22
Twain, Mark, 55

vortex gun, 79

Walker, Samuel, 58-59
war, 12
  antiaircraft guns, 77-79
  balloon guns, 75
  casualties, 45, 71, 76-77
  fire tubes, 16-17
  flintlock muskets, 30-31
  guns and, 19, 31-34, 63, 69, 71
  hand cannons, 18-19
  long-range guns, 75-77
  machine guns, 69, 71-74
  muskets, 22-23, 26-27, 30-31, 40-41, 45
  radar, 80-81
  rifles, 44-45, 50, 72
War of 1812, 44-45
wheel lock musket, 26
Whitney, Eli, 48
witchcraft, 13-14, 16, 33
  fireworks and, 13
  Roger Bacon, 14
World War I, 71, 75-77
World War II, 72-74
  Bofors gun, 78-79
  Paris gun, 76-77
  radar, 80-81

About the Author

Deborah Hitzeroth is a free-lance writer who lives in Virginia. She has a bachelor of arts degree in journalism from the University of Missouri and has completed course work toward a master of arts degree in English. She has worked as a reporter, editor, and free-lance magazine writer. This is her fifth book.

Picture Credits

Cover photo courtesy of MOD Pattern Room, Nottingham

Aberdeen Proving Ground, 79

AP/Wide World Photos, 61 (bottom)

The Cincinnati Historical Society, 45 (bottom)

Culver Pictures, 20, 33

Denver Public Library Western Collection, 65

Department of Defense, 84, 85

Library of Congress, 12, 13, 14 (both), 15, 16, 18, 19, 31, 34, 36 (all), 37 (all), 38, 39, 40, 41 (both), 44 (top left, top right), 45 (top), 47 (top), 49, 50, 54, 58, 61 (top), 64, 67 (bottom), 69, 72, 73 (top), 74 (both), 80

Historical Pictures/Stock Montage, 32

Los Alamos National Laboratory, 83

The Metropolitan Museum of Art, 59 (bottom)

The Metropolitan Museum of Art, Gift of Mrs. Alexander McMillan Welch, 1946, in memory of Alexander McMillan Welch. (46.105), 27

The Metropolitan Museum of Art, Gift of Stephen V. Grancsay, 1942. (42.50.8), 23 (both)

The Metropolitan Museum of Art, Gift of William H. Riggs, 1913. (14.25.1425), 26, 30

The Metropolitan Museum of Art, Harris Brisbane Dick and Rogers Funds, 1987. (1987.274), 29 (both)

The Metropolitan Museum of Art, Rogers Fund, 1910. (10.42), 25 (all)

Benjamin Montag, 42

National Archives, 71 (both), 76, 77 (both), 78 (bottom)

North Wind Picture Archives, 17, 35, 43, 59 (top)

Philippe Plailly/Science Photo Library, 82

Renata Sobieraj, 21, 24, 28, 52, 57, 68, 70

© Smithsonian Institution, 22, 44 (bottom), 46 (both), 47 (bottom), 48 (top), 51 (top), 55 (both), 56, 60, 66, 67 (top), 73 (bottom), 78 (top)

West Point Museum, 51 (bottom), 63